Improve Your Grammar

Study Skills

Academic Success
Academic Writing Skills for International Students
Ace Your Exam
Becoming a Critical Thinker
Be Well, Learn Well
Brilliant Essays
The Business Student's Phrase Book
Cite Them Right (11th edn)
Critical Thinking and Persuasive Writing for Postgraduates
Critical Thinking for Nursing, Health and Social Care
Critical Thinking Skills (3rd edn)
Dissertations and Project Reports
Doing Projects and Reports in Engineering
The Employability Journal
Essentials of Essay Writing
The Exam Skills Handbook (2nd edn)
Get Sorted
The Graduate Career Guidebook (2nd edn)
Great Ways to Learn Anatomy and Physiology (2nd edn)

How to Use Your Reading in Your Essays (3rd edn)
How to Write Better Essays (4th edn)
How to Write Your Literature Review
How to Write Your Undergraduate Dissertation (3rd edn)
Improve Your Grammar (3rd edn)
The Bloomsbury Student Planner
Mindfulness for Students
Presentation Skills for Students (3rd edn)
The Principles of Writing in Psychology
Professional Writing (4th edn)
Reading at University
Reflective Writing for Nursing, Health and Social Work
Simplify Your Study
Skills for Business and Management
Skills for Success (4th edn)
Stand Out from the Crowd
The Student Phrase Book (2nd edn)
The Student's Guide to Writing (3rd edn)

The Study Skills Handbook (5th edn)
Study Skills for International Postgraduates (2nd edn)
Studying in English
Studying Law (4th edn)
The Study Success Journal
Success in Academic Writing (2nd edn)
Smart Thinking
Teaching Study Skills and Supporting Learning
The Undergraduate Research Handbook (2nd edn)
The Work-Based Learning Student Handbook (3rd edn)
Writing for Biomedical Sciences Students
Writing for Engineers (4th edn)
Writing for Nursing and Midwifery Students (3rd edn)
Write it Right (2nd edn)
Writing for Science Students
Writing Skills for Education Students
Writing Skills for Social Work Students
You2Uni: Decide, Prepare, Apply

Pocket Study Skills

14 Days to Exam Success (2nd edn)
Analyzing a Case Study
Brilliant Writing Tips for Students
Completing Your PhD
Doing Research (2nd edn)
Getting Critical (3rd edn)
How to Analyze Data
Managing Stress
Planning Your Dissertation (2nd edn)

Planning Your Essay (3rd edn)
Planning Your PhD
Posters and Presentations
Reading and Making Notes (2nd edn)
Referencing and Understanding Plagiarism (2nd edn)
Reflective Writing (2nd edn)
Report Writing (2nd edn)

Science Study Skills
Studying with Dyslexia (2nd edn)
Success in Groupwork (2nd edn)
Successful Applications
Time Management
Using Feedback to Boost Your Grades
Where's Your Argument?
Where's Your Evidence?
Writing for University (3rd edn)

50 Ways

50 Ways to Boost Your Grades
50 Ways to Boost Your Employability
50 Ways to Excel at Writing

50 Ways to Manage Stress
50 Ways to Manage Time Effectively
50 Ways to Succeed as an International Student

Research Skills

Authoring a PhD
The Foundations of Research (3rd edn)
Getting to Grips with Doctoral Research
Getting Published
The Good Supervisor (2nd edn)

The Lean PhD
Maximizing the Impacts of Academic Research
PhD by Published Work
The PhD Viva
The PhD Writing Handbook
Planning Your Postgraduate Research

The Postgraduate's Guide to Research Ethics
The Postgraduate Research Handbook (2nd edn)
The Professional Doctorate
Structuring Your Research Thesis

For a complete listing of all our titles in this area please visit https://www.bloomsbury.com/uk/academic/study-skills

Improve Your Grammar

The Essential Guide to Accurate Writing

Third Edition

Vanessa Jakeman

Mark Harrison

Ken Paterson

BLOOMSBURY ACADEMIC
LONDON · NEW YORK · OXFORD · NEW DELHI · SYDNEY

BLOOMSBURY ACADEMIC
Bloomsbury Publishing Plc
50 Bedford Square, London, WC1B 3DP, UK
1385 Broadway, New York, NY 10018, USA
29 Earlsfort Terrace, Dublin 2, Ireland

BLOOMSBURY, BLOOMSBURY ACADEMIC and the Diana logo are trademarks
of Bloomsbury Publishing Plc

First published in Great Britain 2012
This edition published 2022
Reprinted 2022

A catalogue record for this book is available from the British Library.

Library of Congress Cataloging-in-Publication Data
Names: Harrison, Mark, 1955– author. | Jakeman, Vanessa author. | Paterson, Ken, 1958– author.
Title: Improve your grammar : the essential guide to accurate writing /
Mark Harrison, Vanessa Jakeman, Ken Paterson.
Description: Third edition. | London ; New York : Bloomsbury Academic, 2022. |
Series: Bloomsbury study skills | Includes index. |
Summary: "Featuring clear guidance, plenty of examples, and short, targeted exercises in
every unit, this guide is all a student needs to master the nuts and bolts of English grammar
and tackle their written assignments with confidence"– Provided by publisher.
Identifiers: LCCN 2021047534 (print) | LCCN 2021047535
Subjects: LCSH: English language–Grammar–Handbooks, manuals, etc.
Classification: LCC PE1112 .H34 2022 (print) | LCC PE1112 (ebook) | DDC 428.2–dc23
LC record available at https://lccn.loc.gov/2021047534
LC ebook record available at https://lccn.loc.gov/2021047535

ISBN: HB: 978-1-3509-3362-0
         PB: 978-1-3509-3363-7
       ePDF: 978-1-3509-3365-1
      eBook: 978-1-3509-3364-4

Series: Bloomsbury Study Skills

Typeset by Integra Software Services Pvt. Ltd.
Printed and bound in Great Britain by Bell and Bain Ltd, Glasgow

To find out more about our authors and books visit www.bloomsbury.com
and sign up for our newsletters.

*The authors would like to
dedicate this book to Morgan Terry.*

Contents

- not since/not until/only when (*Not until/Only when the economy improved did their popularity begin to rise.*)
- neither … nor
- no matter how/what/who, etc. (*No matter how hard they tried, they could not improve the economy.*)
- no, no one, nothing + positive verb (*The policy pleased no one.*)
- any, anyone, anything + negative verb (*The policy did not please anyone.*)
- double negatives

- nouns with compound adjectives (*state-run organisations*)
- nouns with 'that...' clauses (*discuss the view that the plan was not feasible*)

► Key punctuation

► Connections within sentences

- using parallel structures and appropriate punctuation
- presenting points in separate sentences rather than one long sentence

Introduction

What is *Improve Your Grammar*?

Improve Your Grammar is a study and practice book for students attending or planning to attend university or college. It concentrates on the specific areas of grammar, vocabulary and coherence where students frequently make mistakes, and deals with these in a straightforward, accessible way.

The units feature:

- clear, jargon-free explanations
- a consistent focus on key grammar and coherence
- examples of typical student errors, with corrections
- tips and advice
- a realistic academic context across a range of subject areas
- easy-to-use practice exercises, with answers.

What are the book's aims?

Improve Your Grammar aims to:

- correct students' grammatical mistakes
- encourage students to write in an appropriate academic style
- extend students' range of expression
- help students to break out of bad habits

and thereby **improve overall performance** in their subject areas.

What kind of problems does it deal with?

Improve Your Grammar addresses common problems experienced by a large number of students, such as:

- writing sentences that are grammatically incorrect or incomplete
- using punctuation incorrectly
- using incorrect verb forms
- failing to connect sentences in an appropriate way

- making mistakes in word choice and spelling
- writing long and confusing sentences
- writing in an inappropriate register
- writing in a simplistic style.

How is the book organised?

Improve Your Grammar is divided into 62 units, grouped in sections that cover:

- grammar terminology
- key grammatical areas
- punctuation
- ways of connecting sentences
- ways of producing good sentences
- key areas and features of academic writing
- vocabulary and spelling.

The contents of the book are presented in **double-page spreads** making it easy to navigate when looking for a particular item or section.

The **first part** of each unit explains the area being covered as simply as possible, with examples of mistakes and how to correct them.

Key information is highlighted in **Writing Tip** boxes, which explain how the unit is relevant to academic work; **Danger Zone** boxes, highlighting very common problem areas; **Rules** boxes, laying down practices that must be followed; and **Remember!** boxes providing essential notes.

The **second part** of each unit contains carefully-focused practice exercises (for which answers are given at the end of the book), allowing users to check their understanding immediately.

The units build on each other to cover the principal areas that are essential for students. 'Connections within sentences', for example, contains a series of four linked units focusing on the language required for 'contrasting' and 'adding' information and for describing 'causes' and 'results'.

How to use this book

As a student

This is an invaluable **reference** and **practice book** that will help you improve the accuracy and quality of your writing. Use the **contents** and the **index** pages to help you find the sections that are relevant to your needs.

Here are some typical questions that students ask and the units in the book that help answer them:

What's a sentence? Why do I make mistakes writing complete sentences?	**Unit 2** is all about the rules for forming a sentence. It illustrates different types of clause and shows how these can be combined into a sentence. It also explains the meaning of terms such as *subject*, *verb* and *object*.
What's the difference between 'its' and 'it is'? When do I need to use an apostrophe?	**Unit 23** focuses on apostrophes. The Danger Zone explains the difference between '*its*' and '*it is*' and also discusses areas of confusion, such as *their* and *they're*.
How can I vary the way I make comparisons?	**Units 16** and **17** provide lots of examples of how to use a range of words and phrases to make comparisons, and also to contrast and show differences.
What different ways are there of stating conclusions?	**Unit 48** includes a section on drawing conclusions and making recommendations. A sample paragraph illustrates some of the various ways of doing this.
What is hedging and why does it matter?	**Units 39** and **40** explain why hedging is used in academic writing and provide examples of different ways of using hedging language.
What's a verb and what's an adverb? What's a linking word or phrase?	**Unit 1** explains and illustrates all the different parts of speech, such as *verbs*, *nouns*, *adjectives* and linking words.
What is the passive and when should I use it?	**Unit 7**, on using the passive, tells you how the passive is formed and why it is used. It also has a section on using the passive with reporting verbs such as *argue* and *claim*.
What's the difference between 'written' and 'had written'? When should I use 'had' before a verb?	**Unit 5** explains when to use different verb tenses. Point 2 in this unit provides examples of phrases that are often followed by the past perfect tense (*had written*).

When your tutor gives you feedback on your writing, note their comments then check the **index** for the appropriate page in this book.

New media may be winning the battle, but old media will always have its advocates, states Hammond.

HJP 25/2/2021 09:07   ✕
Comment [1]: This is a direct quote from Hammond–you need to paraphrase it.

Index extract:

paraphrasing strategies **90–91**

As a tutor

This is the ideal book for teachers who are supporting students with their writing. It can be used **in the classroom** or for **self-study**, and references to specific units can be incorporated into the **essay feedback** that you give.

Here is an essay extract written by a first-year student on a BA Politics course. The tutor has commented on some of the errors and directed the student to the relevant sections of the book:

Equality is a concept which effects societies on a political, social and economic level. There are many forms of equality which challenge socialist and liberal thinkers. Equality of outcome is one of three main forms of equality which arises out of egalitarian discourse. Equality of outcome is a more radical approach to liberal thought; it looks at the end results of an outcome, rather than initial circumstances which arise at the beginning of life. It doesn't matter what position you are born at in life, progression over the years will lead to literal equality among all. Rousseau quotes "no citizen shall be rich enough to buy another and none so poor as to be forced to sell himself". Here Rousseau sees the danger of social inequality and how material wealth can lead to the rich not only becoming selfish but they also fail to understand that redistribution of wealth is needed to reduce social inequalities.

HJP 25/2/2021 08:15
Comment [1]: 'affects' – see p116, 'Commonly misused words'

HJP 25/2/2021 08:16
Comment [2]: 'arise' – see p8, subject/verb agreement

HJP 25/2/2021 08:16
Comment [3]: Incorrect introduction of quote. See Unit 43, 'Citing'

HJP 25/2/2021 08:16
Comment [4]: Not a correct sentence. Use two sentences or parallel clauses – see Unit 33, 'Parallel Structures'

Alternatively, this book can be used as a **teaching tool** for all types of **academic English courses and modules,** pre-sessional and in-sessional. The structure of the book allows it to be used in different ways, and the coverage of grammar in its widest sense makes it invaluable for students at all levels of proficiency and from a wide range of subject areas.

You may choose to:

- suggest that students read units at home, without doing the exercises, then run through these in class to check understanding (particularly useful for the first section on **Key terms**);
- use one of the exercises provided as a controlled practice test to help students self-assess before covering material in the units;
- ask the class to work in pairs or groups on specific units in the book, while you take feedback queries from students on an individual basis;
- refer individual students to relevant units in the book;

- spend short, but regular, periods of time each week focusing on the units most relevant to your students;
- focus on your students' writing at the sentence level, using the sections on **Key terms** and **Producing good sentences**;
- use the units in **Features of writing** to help students write more coherently and develop an academic style;
- use the sections on **Connections within sentences** and **Features of writing** to help your students write in a clear, well-structured manner;
- enhance your students' lexical resource by selecting relevant units from the section on **Using the right words**;
- ask students to write their own sample sentences or paragraphs that include features covered in the units you have studied together;
- train students to improve their own writing by using the very detailed **index** and **contents** pages to locate specific concerns.

1 Parts of speech

Nouns

A **noun** is a word used for a thing or a person:
book, tutor

Many nouns can be singular or plural:
source, sources

Some nouns are called 'uncountable' because they cannot be used in a plural form:
education, health

Verbs

- A **verb** is a word used for an action or a state:
write, think

- A verb **tense** is the form of a verb used for the present, the past or the future:
wrote, will write, was thinking
  ◗ See **4** *Correct tense formation*.

- An **auxiliary** is a form of the verbs 'to be' or 'to have' that is used to create some verb tenses:
has given, **was** thinking

An auxiliary is also used for forming negative verbs:
did not happen, **are not** working
and questions:
did it happen? **have** they seen it?

- A **modal** verb goes with another verb to express various ideas or shades of meaning. Modal verbs are **may**, **might**, **can**, **could**, **should**, **must**, **ought to**, **would**, **will**, **shall**:
should happen, would not have happened, might be changing
  ◗ See **6** *Modal verbs*.

- A **participle** is a form of a verb used in various verb tenses.
A **present participle** ends with '-ing':
am think**ing**, was work**ing**
A **regular past participle** ends with '-ed' or '-d':
research → had research**ed**, announce → have announce**d**
Some past participles are **irregular**:
give → have **given**, think → had **thought**,
  ◗ See **34** *Participles*.

- An **infinitive** is 'to' + verb:
to improve, to conclude

- A **gerund** is a form of a verb ending with '-ing':
start **improving**, therefore **concluding**
  ◗ See **13** *Gerunds and infinitives*.

Adjectives

- An **adjective** describes the appearance or nature of something:
long, difficult
An adjective goes together with a noun:
a **difficult** question

- A **possessive adjective** indicates that something belongs to or is connected with someone or something:
my, your, its, his, her, our, their

Adverbs

An **adverb** describes how something happens or is done:
quickly, carefully
An adverb goes together with a verb:
think **carefully**
An adverb can also go with an adjective:
really beautiful
  ◗ See **10** *Using adverbs*.

Prepositions

A **preposition** is a word or phrase such as:
at, of, in, on, for, off, out of, from, by, with
Prepositions are used in many ways, for example in connection with time (on Tuesday), place (in paragraph 2) or movement (out of the door), and also in many phrases (off duty, in common). Prepositions are used after verbs, nouns and adjectives to form phrases with particular meanings:
look at a report, take an **interest in**, feel **proud of**
  ◗ See **50** and **51** *Using prepositions*.

Pronouns

A **pronoun** is a word that is used instead of a noun or name to refer to people and things.
Most pronouns are called **personal pronouns**, and they are in various categories:

subject pronouns → I, you, he, she, it, we, they
possessive pronouns → mine, yours, its, ours, theirs

Other words can also be used as pronouns, for example this, that, these, those

⏵ See **31** *Using pronouns correctly* and **32** *Avoiding repetition of words.*

Articles

Articles are the words **a/an** and **the**, which are used before nouns:

a review, an essay, the course

⏵ See **14** *Articles.*

Linking words and phrases

Words and phrases that join parts of sentences together are sometimes called **conjunctions**, **connectives** or **linkers**.
Examples of linking words and phrases are:
and, but, or
because (of), as, since, due to, as a result (of), when, while, until, as soon as, once
if, unless, as long as, provided that, even if
as well as, in addition (to), furthermore
although, even though, despite, however

⏵ See **26, 27, 28** and **29** *Linking.*

Exercises

1 List the words used in the sentences below according to their parts of speech.

The course provides a useful qualification and graduates regularly find positions in a variety of professions. Full details are available on our website. Furthermore, we operate an advisory service so that prospective students can quickly get clear answers to their queries.

Nouns:..

....

Verbs:...

Adjectives:...

Adverbs:...

Prepositions:...

Pronouns:..

Articles:..

Linking words/phrases:...

2 Match the underlined words with the verb forms 1–6.

a When you have <u>completed</u> the application form, send it to the address below.
b Your personal statement <u>should</u> include any information relevant to your application.
c It is important <u>to study</u> the entry requirements carefully.
d If you are <u>considering</u> this course, go to page 23 for more information.
e Applications <u>must</u> be received before the closing date.
f Our students enjoy <u>relaxing</u> in the leisure facilities on campus.
g Overseas students <u>do</u> not have to fill in this section.

1 auxiliary
2 modal
3 present participle

4 past participle
5 infinitive
6 gerund

2 Parts of a sentence

A sentence is a group of words with one or more 'clauses'. It begins with a capital letter and ends with a full stop, a question mark or an exclamation mark. A sentence can be short or long.

 Writing Tip

Understanding how a sentence works will help you to produce grammatically accurate writing.

Subject + verb (+ object)

- A sentence must have a **subject** and a **verb** that is connected with it.

subject   verb

This university   is   very popular.

- A sentence may also have an **object** after the verb.

subject   verb   object of verb

This university   attracts   students   from all over the world.

Clauses

- A sentence contains one or more clauses. It must have a main clause.
- A sentence that contains a main clause and one or more dependent clauses is called a **complex sentence**.
- Clauses are normally separated by commas.

1 Main clause

- A main clause contains a **subject** and a **verb** and makes sense on its own.
- A sentence may consist only of a main clause:

subject   verb   two objects linked by 'and'

The university   has   600 undergraduates and 300 postgraduate students.

2 Co-ordinated clauses

- A sentence may consist of two main clauses, each of which makes sense on its own, linked by a simple conjunction, such as *and*, *but* or *so*. This is called a compound sentence:

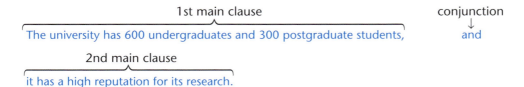

1st main clause   conjunction
                                                        ↓
The university has 600 undergraduates and 300 postgraduate students,   and

2nd main clause

it has a high reputation for its research.

3 Dependent clauses

- A sentence may consist of a main clause and one or more dependent clauses, such as a participle clause or a relative clause.
- The underlined parts of the sentences below are dependent clauses. They could not be presented separately as sentences as they do not make sense on their own.

participle clause   main clause

<u>Founded in 1922,</u> the university has 600 undergraduates and 300 postgraduate students.

▶ See **34** *Participles.*

- Alternatively, a clause may be within another clause:

relative clause

The university,   <u>which was founded in 1922,</u>   has 600 undergraduates and 300 postgraduate students.

▶ See **15** *Relative clauses.*

- A sentence may have more than one dependent clause:
  The department underwent reforms which, although they took a while to take effect, proved successful.
  The main clause   →   The department underwent reforms
  First dependent clause   →   which proved successful.
  Second dependent clause →   although they took a while to take effect

- A dependent clause does not have to have a verb:
  As a result of an increase in applications, the department was expanded.

 **Remember!**
A dependent clause on its own is an incomplete sentence, and is grammatically incorrect.

▶ See **35** *Incomplete sentences.*

Exercises

1 Identify the subject, main verb and object in each of these sentences.

a At some schools, pupils can take the International Baccalaureate.
b When comprehensive schools first opened in the 1950s, many people welcomed them as a big improvement in education.
c Private schools often offer scholarships.

2 Underline the main clause in each of these sentences.

a Students applying for university places have to complete the application process, which includes a personal statement.
b The three categories of state schools during the 1960s were grammar, comprehensive and secondary modern.
c In the 1990s, when polytechnics changed their name and became universities, the overall number of applications for higher education places rose sharply.

3 How many clauses are there in these sentences?

a The system for the funding of higher education, which has changed several times over the past few decades, is a major issue in the UK, affecting a great many families.
b British universities, because of their high reputation, have long attracted overseas students and these students have become an important source of revenue.
c In order to attract students who otherwise might not have gone to a university at all, the variety of courses on offer at British universities has greatly increased over the last two decades.

3 Singular or plural subjects and verbs

A singular subject must have a singular verb:
One member of the panel **was** opposed to the proposal.

A plural subject must have a plural verb:
Most members of the panel **were** in favour of the proposal.

 Writing Tip

Make sure your verbs are correctly singular or plural by identifying their subject. Incorrect verb tenses give a bad impression in academic writing.

Identifying the subject of a verb

In a complex sentence a verb can be a long way from its subject and it is easy to get confused about whether it should be singular or plural.

▶ **Decide what's wrong with the sentences on the left, before looking at the explanations on the right.**

One of the main issues surrounding classrooms from the point of view of teachers are discipline. ✖

→ The word 'issues' is plural but the subject of the verb is 'One' and so the verb must be singular. The sentence is about one issue, 'discipline'.
↓

One of the main issues surrounding classrooms from the point of view of teachers **is** discipline. ✔

A very good example of the kind of approaches that work in these situations are pairwork activities. ✖

→ The phrase 'pairwork activities' is plural, but it is not the subject of the verb. The subject is the singular 'example'.
↓

A very good example of the kind of approaches that work in these situations **is** pairwork activities. ✔

This is one of the many problems that has affected the teaching profession for decades. ✖

→ Although the sentence begins with the singular 'This is', the subject of the verb 'affected' is the plural 'problems'.
↓

This is one of the many **problems** that **have** affected the teaching profession for decades. ✔

The different ability levels of children in a single class obviously has a big effect on the method a teacher chooses to use. ✖

→ The words 'ability' and 'class' are singular but the subject of the verb is the plural 'levels'.
↓

The different ability **levels** of children in a single class obviously **have** a big effect on the method a teacher chooses to use. ✔

Improve Your Grammar

Group nouns

- Group nouns like **police, government, class, crowd, team, public, audience, press, family, community, population** and **staff** may not end with 's' or 'es', but they still have a plural meaning.

- If the word is used to refer to the group as a single unit, use a singular verb:
  A child's **family has** a huge influence on his or her education.

- If the word is used to refer to the various members in the group, use a plural verb:
  The child's **family were** not all living in the same house.

- Note that 'police' is always used with a plural verb:
  The **police** regularly **visit** the school to give talks to the pupils.

- **Everybody**, **everyone**, **nobody** and **no one** must be used with singular verbs:
  Everybody in the teaching profession **is** in agreement about the new policy.

Numbers

- Use a singular verb with '**the** number of' and a plural verb with '**a** (small/large) number of':
  The number of teachers taking career breaks **has** risen significantly in the last three years.
  A number of head teachers **are** paid advisers to other schools in their area.

- With fractions, percentages and proportions, the verb agrees with the noun nearest to it:
  During the summer programme, half/50 per cent of the school **day is** devoted to sports.
  Three-quarters/75 per cent/The majority of the **schools** in the area **have** reported a decline in bullying.

- Note that 'the average' is used with a singular verb:
  The average age of the children participating in the project **is** seven.

 Danger Zone
Is a noun singular or plural?
Academic subjects that end with 's' (e.g. politics, economics) are singular, but when the same word is used with a different meaning not referring to academic study, a plural verb is used:
Economics is an optional subject on the curriculum.
The **economics** of this proposal **make** it impractical.

Exercises

1 Decide whether or not the underlined verbs in these sentences are correct.

a The Government <u>is</u> considering various options for reforming the system.
b Secure parking is one of several issues that <u>has</u> to be addressed urgently by planners.
c Problems that affect both residents and businesses in the area <u>includes</u> traffic congestion.
d Noise pollution is something that a great many people <u>is</u> affected by.
e This is typical of the developments that most <u>concern</u> environmentalists today.
f A common result of management initiatives affecting staff in these ways <u>is</u> industrial disputes.
g This is among the repercussions that <u>is</u> seldom foreseen by any expert.

2 Choose the correct verb form.

a Everybody in those professions with experience of current developments .... (*thinks/think*) that reform is essential.
b The maintenance costs of each single piece of equipment .... (*tends/tend*) to be high.
c Figures indicate that a quarter of UK households now .... (*suffers/suffer*) from fuel poverty.
d Some media commentators suggested that the police .... (*was/were*) responsible for the leak.
e The number of schools reporting a decrease in truancy .... (*has/have*) doubled over the last five years.
f The politics that .... (*surrounds/surround*) this issue make it a very controversial one.
g He was among the Members of Parliament who .... (*was/were*) elected in 2011.

4 Correct tense formation

A verb **tense** is the form of the verb that relates to the time when something happens.
For example, there are different tenses for **present** actions:

New research **is changing** current thinking.
present continuous for ongoing actions = now

Research **is** vital for the development of counselling practice.
present simple for present states, truths, etc. = always

💡 Writing Tip

Using correct verb tenses relies on an understanding of the time reference(s) in every sentence that you write.

Past simple (I did it) and present perfect (I have done it)

▶ **Look at these incorrect sentences and consider why the underlined verb tenses are wrong.**

Since the 1980s, an increasing number of people in the UK <u>did</u> courses enabling them to practise as counsellors. ✘
Two decades ago, the number of professionals involved in counselling <u>has grown</u> suddenly. ✘

What's wrong: The choice of tense must match the time that is being referred to in the sentence.

🔀 Rules

Use the **past simple** tense if you are referring to a time in the past and talking about something that was completed at that time.
Use the **present perfect** tense when the time mentioned includes the past and the present.

● Here are the incorrect sentences above with the correct tenses:

<u>Since the 1980s</u>, an increasing number of people in the UK **have done** courses enabling them to practise as counsellors. ✔	→	The phrase 'Since the 1980s' refers to a period of time that includes the present, so the **present perfect** is required.
<u>Two decades ago</u>, the number of professionals involved in counselling **grew** suddenly. ✔	→	The phrase 'Two decades ago' refers to the past only, so the **past simple** is required.

Continuous verb tenses

<u>At that time</u>, counsellors **were dealing with** the situation for the first time.	→	The **past continuous** (*was/were + '-ing'*) describes an action or situation continuing at a particular point in the past.
The training course for counsellors **has been running** <u>for two years now</u>.	→	The **present perfect continuous** (*have/has + been + '-ing'*) is used for something continuing for a period of time starting in the past and still happening now.

Past perfect simple (I had done) and past perfect continuous (I had been doing)

By 1990, the number of trained counsellors **had risen** significantly.

→ The **past perfect** (*had + past participle*) refers to something that happened before or until a particular time in the past.

Prior to this date, many people **had been suffering** on their own with mental health problems.

→ The **past perfect continuous** (*had been + '-ing'*) is used for something that continued for a period of time before a particular point in the past.

 Danger Zone

We was/He done it

Some people use incorrect verb tenses when they are talking, but never do this when you are writing.

We was talking about … ✖   They was right when they said … ✖

- Remember that 'we' and 'they' are plural and are followed by 'were', not 'was'.
  We were talking about … ✔ **They were right** when they said … ✔

He done it very well. ✖

- This verb form does not exist. There are two possible correct forms:
  He **did** it very well. ✔   if you are talking about something completely in the past.
  He **has done** it very well. ✔   if you are talking about something with a connection to the present.

Special uses of tenses in academic writing

- The present simple is often used to report research results, discuss the arguments of other academics and to summarise articles, chapters, etc.
  Both studies **conclude** that …; As Browne **explains**, …; The Benson Report **considers** the effects of …
  ◢ See **43** *Citing*.

- The present perfect is used for research/arguments that began in the past and are ongoing.
  Many scientists **have explored** the issue, but they **have been unable** to reach a consensus on it.

- The past simple is used to describe reports on the procedure in particular experiments/studies.
  Peters **interviewed** 66 survivors who had undergone counselling.

Exercises

1 Decide whether or not the underlined verb tenses are correct, and correct those that are not.

a In recent times, new evidence pointing to the real causes of this problem <u>has emerged</u>.
b It was at that point that the benefits of radical reform of the system <u>have become</u> apparent.
c Since then, numerous studies <u>supported</u> this theory.
d At the start of this decade, nobody <u>foresaw</u> these developments.
e Back then, few experts <u>have realised</u> the importance of these findings.

2 Complete this paragraph by circling the correct verb tenses.

One of the main appeals of any new technology is the novelty value that it (a) *has/is having*. When mobile phones, for example, (b) *was/were* new and expensive, owners (c) *liked/were liking* to display them to impress others. After they (d) *have been using/had been using* them for a while, however, the novelty (e) *wore/has worn* off. In the mid 1990s, not many people (f) *were owning/owned* a mobile phone, but by the early 2000s, most people (g) *had bought/bought* one and (h) *were using/have been using* it regularly. Nowadays, mobile phones (i) *became/have become* part of everyday life and newer, more exciting developments (j) *were attracting/are attracting* the attention of the general public.

5   Using more than one verb tense

In July last year, an experiment **was set up**, in
which different groups of participants who **had not
previously met** and who **had not received** any
preparation, **answered** questions while they **were
dealing** with a number of different tasks.

► Look at the underlined verb tenses in these incorrect sentences from reports on research.

1   Incorrectly mixing past and present tenses

The groups went into separate rooms so that they <u>can't</u> hear each other. ✖

What's wrong: Both actions took place in the past and so the second verb tense is wrong.
The groups **went** into separate rooms so that they **couldn't** hear each other. ✔

2   Describing one past action that followed another past action

Once they <u>completed</u> the tasks in Room A, the groups went into Room B.

What's wrong: The past perfect, describing an earlier action, should be used in the first part of the sentence:
Once they **had completed** the tasks in Room A, the groups **went** into Room B. ✔

Other time words and phrases that operate in the same way as 'once' include 'when', 'as soon as' and
'after':
<u>When</u>/<u>As soon as</u>/<u>After</u> they **had completed** the first task, the group **went on** to do the second task. ✔

3   Misusing the present perfect tense

The results showed that the second group <u>have done</u> the tasks better than the first. ✖

What's wrong: The present perfect ('have done') cannot be used to talk about something that is completely
in the past. Use the past perfect or the past simple instead:
The results **showed** that the second group **had done** (or **did**) the task better than the first. ✔

4   Describing something that is generally true

People who adopt that approach to the task <u>are always doing</u> it well. ✖

What's wrong: Both verbs, 'adopt' and 'do', describe something that is generally true, so they should **both**
be in the present simple:
People who **adopt** that approach to the task always **do** it well. ✔

5   Reporting speech

Researchers told all the participants that they <u>have done</u> very well. ✖

What's wrong: When you are reporting what someone said in the past, you need to change the tense of
the verb that the person used when speaking. In this case, the speaker said 'You've done very well.'
Researchers **told** all the participants that they **had done** very well. ✔

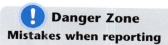 **Danger Zone**

Mistakes when reporting

In spoken language an incorrect tense for reporting may not matter, but in academic work it is inappropriate.

The researchers claimed that their study means that common beliefs on the subject are wrong.

The researchers **claimed** that their study **meant** that common beliefs on the subject **were** wrong. ✔

Reporting information in academic writing

The following tense changes are made when reporting information:

	The researchers reported that ...
The results **look** remarkably consistent. →	the results **looked** remarkably consistent.
We **are analysing** the results. →	they **were analysing** the results.
The experiments **were** successful. →	the experiments **had been** successful.
We **have formed** certain conclusions. →	they **had formed** certain conclusions.
The results **will** have important effects. →	the results **would** have important effects.

Exercises

1 Decide whether or not the underlined verb tenses in these sentences are correct, and correct those that are not.

a It was clear that the situation <u>could not continue</u> and that something had to be done as a matter of urgency.

b When the researchers <u>analysed</u> all the evidence, they formed their conclusions.

c They presented the data so that a non-expert <u>can understand</u> it.

d The poem was a new direction for him because <u>he had not written</u> in that style before.

e He wrote about subjects that still <u>have</u> relevance for people today.

f After people <u>came</u> to terms with the shock of this event, they began to adapt to the new circumstances.

2 Complete the reported statements.

a The report stated: 'Fish are returning to the river now that it is unpolluted.'
  The report stated that ....

b 'I will stay in office until the board has appointed a successor,' he announced.
  He announced that ....

c A spokesman said: 'We are investigating the problem but have not found the cause yet.'
  A spokesman said that ....

d An official statement declared: 'The talks were successful and we hope to sign an agreement.'
  An official statement declared that ....

e A government report predicted: 'Until exports rise, economic growth will not return.'
  A government report predicted that ....

f 'I cannot comment because I do not know the details of the case,' the spokeswoman replied.
  The spokeswoman replied that ....

6 Modal verbs

Modal verbs are used before other verbs to express various meanings such as possibilities and obligations.

Can, **could**, **may**, **might**, **must**, **need**, **ought to** and **should** are modal verbs.

Fashion imagery **may promote** extreme dieting among some young people.

Should and must

- You can use **should** to express two meanings:

  1. 'It's a good idea'
     Products **should be** attractive as well as functional.
     With this meaning, *should* is weaker than *must*.

  2. 'It's likely'
     The exhibition **should attract** a wide audience because the drawings are unique.
     With this meaning, *should* is stronger than *may/might/could*.

- You can use **must** to express two meanings:

  1. 'It is necessary'
     Designs for public buildings **must take into account** the needs of all the users.
     The negative forms **must not** and **do not have to** have different meanings:
     Visitors to the gallery ~~do not have to~~ **must not touch** the exhibits. (= it's not allowed)
     Visitors to the gallery ~~must not~~ **do not have to pay**, but can make a donation. (= it's optional)
     The past form is **had to**:
     The exhibition was so popular that timed tickets **had to be issued**.

  2. 'This is the logical conclusion'
     Some of the missing ceramics **must be** in private collections.
     Bacon **must have destroyed** some of his early paintings.
     The negative forms are **cannot + verb** for the present and **cannot/could not have + past participle** for the past:
     Stevens argues that estimations of the cost of restoring the building **cannot be** correct.
     Vince Green **could not have known** that Stella Law was working on exactly the same designs.

Ought to

Ought to is less common than *should*, but means exactly the same.

- Present: **ought to/ought not to + verb**
  Theatre designs **ought not to distract** the audience from the meaning of the play.
- Past: **ought to have/ought not to have + past participle**
  The reproductions in the catalogue **ought to have been** larger.

 **Danger Zone**

Should of/Would of/Could of/Must of

In spoken English *have* may sound like *of*, but it is never correct to write *of* as part of a past modal form.

In a different economic climate, sales of the new designs would ~~of~~ **have** been better.
Without that piece of good fortune, she might not ~~of~~ **have** become such a well-known designer.

Problems with past forms

1 Incorrect use of 'could'

After extensive negotiations, BJ Separates could make an exclusive agreement with CTY Designs. ✖

→ **What's wrong**: You cannot use *could* for a specific achievement in the past.

↓

After extensive negotiations, BJ Separates **was able to** make/**managed to** make/**succeeded in** making an exclusive agreement with CTY Designs. ✔

2 Did not need to/need not have

Juny Patterns Ltd did not need to go bankrupt if they had restricted their business to the UK. ✖

→ **What's wrong**: *Did not need to* + verb is used for things that **did not** happen (because they were not necessary).

↓

The clients **did not need to secure** a loan in order to set up Elig Suits as they had sufficient savings. ✔

NOTE: *Need not have* + past participle is used for things that did happen (but they were not necessary).

→ Juny Patterns Ltd **need not have gone** bankrupt if they had restricted their business to the UK. ✔

3 Incorrect use of 'must not have'

The designer handbags on sale at £25 each must not have been genuine. ✖

→ **What's wrong**: To express the opposite of *must have been*, you need to use *cannot* or *could not have been*.

↓

The designer handbags on sale at £25 each **cannot/could not have been** genuine. ✔

Exercises

1 Write the correct option in the space.

a Valto Dresses managed to save money because it .... (*did not need to open/need not have opened*) an office in Paris.

b FJY Style Ltd .... (*must have released/had to release*) a statement in March 2020, saying that its factories did not employ workers on twenty-hour shifts.

c Sue Cape .... (*must not/cannot*) be the first jeweller to work exclusively in Welsh gold, but she is making a reputation as the most interesting.

d Had he made a full apology, designer Tom Gott .... (*did not need to resign/need not have resigned*).

e Foster .... (*must have been working/must have worked*) on the painting when he died, because the half-finished canvas was found in his studio.

f The new range of cosmetics .... (*should/can*) sell well next year in Japan.

2 Correct the use of modal verbs in each of these sentences.

a Dalio's work in sculpture must not have been a success because she soon turned to painting.

b With a more attractive design, the product could of become a brand leader.

c Critics argued that the gallery ought to have not allowed the painting to be sold to a museum.

d Fortunately, the organisers could save the show by using a back-up generator.

7   Using the passive

Verbs can be in the **active** or **passive** form.

> An **active** verb is used when the subject 'does' the verb:
> The **voters** of Merthyr Tydfil **elected** Keir Hardie as the first
> Labour Party MP in 1900.

The subject is 'voters' and they 'elected'.

> A **passive** verb is used when the subject does not 'do' the verb:
> **Keir Hardie was elected** as the first Labour MP by the voters of
> Merthyr Tydfil in 1900.

The subject is '*Keir Hardie*' but he did not '*elect*' – the voters '*elected*'. The passive makes Keir Hardie the main focus of the sentence, not the voters.

 Writing Tip

The passive allows you to keep the important element in your writing at the beginning of a sentence or clause. Using the passive can also help you to achieve the impersonal style that academic writing normally requires.

 Rules

The passive is made using a form of the verb *be* + past participle (*designed*, *taken*, etc.). Here are examples in the main tenses, and in the modal, gerund and infinitive forms:

A candidate **is chosen** by a constituency party.   *active: they choose a candidate*
The televising of trials **is** currently **being discussed**.   *active: they are discussing*
A new political party **has been established.**   *active: they have established*
David Cameron **was elected** to Parliament in 2001.   *active: they elected David Cameron*
The offender **was being taken** to jail when he escaped.   *active: they were taking*
After a ceasefire **had been agreed**, fighting stopped.   *active: they had agreed*
New immigrants **will be given** an English test.   *active: they will give*
A recount **may be held** because the vote was so close. (*modal*)   *active: they may hold a recount*
MPs do not like **being criticised** by their own party. (*gerund*)   *active: they do not like their own party criticising them*

Sara Kemp hopes **to be confirmed** as the new candidate. (*infinitive*)   *active: hopes they will confirm her*

▶ **Read these sentences and the reasons for using the passive.**

At that time, reforms to the voting system **were being brought in** by the new Government.	→	Used to make the important thing ('reforms') the main focus, rather than the people ('the new Government') who did them.
Her application to become an MP **has been rejected.**	→	The writer does not know who did the action.
The protestors **were** all **sentenced** to six months in prison.	→	It is not worth mentioning who did the action because it is obvious (a judge).
It **is believed** that rebel forces used the internet to plan their campaign.	→	The writer is putting across a view or claim that may not be fact. (See '**Passives with reporting verbs below**')

▶ Read this paragraph, and note how the writer uses passives to keep 'the Palace of Westminster' as the main focus.

> The Palace of Westminster comprises the House of Commons and the House of Lords. It **was designed** by Charles Barry in Gothic style, and **completed** in 1870, after a number of delays. In 1987 the Palace **was declared** a 'World Heritage Site' by UNESCO.

Passives with reporting verbs in academic writing

Passive forms of reporting verbs such as *believe, claim, know, report, say, think* and *understand* are sometimes used to depersonalise claims, to give a more academic tone to a piece of writing.

There are two patterns:

- It + be + *believed/said*, etc. + that …
  It was known that Winston Churchill suffered from short periods of depression.
  It is **thought that** translation services are costing the European Union more than €1bn a year.

- Noun + be + *believed/said*, etc. + present/past/continuous infinitive …
  Winston Churchill **is known to have suffered from** short periods of depression.
  Translation services **are thought to be costing** the European Union more than €1bn a year.

Remember!

You do not need to say who did something when using the passive:

Bills are **read, debated** and often **amended** before being passed into law.

⬧ See **33** *Parallel structures.*

Exercises

1 Rewrite these sentences, starting with the underlined part.
   a Former American President Jimmy Carter won <u>the Nobel Peace Prize</u> in 2002.
   b MPs will debate <u>the Bill</u> later in the week.
   c A clerk was destroying <u>the documents</u> when the police arrived.
   d The Government might postpone <u>the referendum</u>.
   e Protestors have occupied <u>three government buildings</u>.
   f Rioters had stolen <u>most of the museum's collection</u> by the time the army arrived.

2 Rewrite these sentences in two ways using reporting verbs.
   a Commentators believe that Walter Clark is the Senate's most skilful debater.
      It ....
      Walter Clark ....
   b A journalist reported that two politicians took bribes for their votes.
      It ....
      Two politicians ....
   c Officials say that talks are taking place between the two parties.
      It ....
      Talks ....
   d People think that Che Guevara was executed to avoid the drama of a trial.
      It ....
      Che Guevara ....

8 Direct and indirect questions

A **direct question** is a *question* that is actually asked. It has a question mark at the end of it.

What can we conclude from the evidence?

 Writing Tip

In formal, academic writing, indirect questions are more commonly used than direct questions, although direct questions can be effective at times. It is important to use both types of question correctly.

An **indirect question** is a *statement* that is based on a direct question that was asked or could be asked. The statement ends with a full stop.

We must decide **what we can conclude** from the evidence.

▶ Read this paragraph from an essay about laws and look at the direct (1) and indirect (2) questions in it. Look at the punctuation too.

> One of the fundamental issues surrounding the introduction of any new law is this: **is it possible to enforce it? (1)** Lawmakers know that they have to work out **how to ensure that (2)** people adhere to the new law, and they have to ask themselves: **what they need to consider (2)** in order to make certain that this law has a realistic chance of being effective. They need to be absolutely clear as to **how the authorities will enforce it (2)**. With attempts to legislate in connection with the internet, this fundamental issue is particularly pertinent. **How can such legislation work? (1)** There might be general agreement on **why such laws are required (2)** but enforcement is almost impossible to guarantee.

Direct questions

Some direct questions ask for the answer '**Yes**' or '**No**' → *Is it possible?*
Some direct questions ask for **information** → *What do we need?*

A direct question can be formed with these patterns:

 Remember!

Asking a direct question about an issue can be an effective way of introducing an opinion or view on it.

- the verb 'be' + subject:
  Is it possible to enforce it?

- a modal verb (can, should, will, etc.) + subject + main verb:
  How **can such legislation work**?

- an auxiliary (do, does, have, had, etc.) + subject + main verb:
  What **do we need** to consider … ?

Improve Your Grammar

Indirect questions

These questions do not have the same word order as direct questions because they are phrased as statements.

Direct question → *Is it possible?*
Indirect question → *They need to know if/whether it is possible.*

An indirect question can be formed with these patterns:

- question word + subject + verb:
  They need to be absolutely clear as to **how the authorities will enforce** it.
  There might be general agreement on **why such laws are required** but ...

- question word + 'to' infinitive (not used with 'why'):
  ... they have to work out **how to ensure** that people ...

 Remember!

You can often use 'if' or 'whether' when there is no other question word to use:

Do people support the law?

The authorities are not sure **whether** people support the law.

ⓘ Danger Zone
Incorrect phrasing of indirect questions

An indirect question is a statement, not a question. It uses the same word order for subject, verb, etc. as any other statement:

We need to know <u>what experts regard</u> as the most serious legal issues surrounding the internet. ✔
We need to know what do experts regard as the ... ✘

Exercises

1 Decide whether these indirect questions are written correctly, and correct the ones that are not.

a It was hard for legislators at the time to foresee what would the effects of this law be.
b It is instructive to examine why it took so long for the issue to be addressed.
c Things change and at times it is necessary to ask whether certain laws should be modified to accommodate those changes.
d Experts need to co-operate in order to determine exactly how can a new law be implemented.
e Many professionals are still finding out how does the internet affect them from a professional point of view.
f Creating the law is one thing, but nobody knows how much harder it will be to enforce it.
g The public should be clear about whether or not have they broken the law.

2 Complete the indirect questions.

a Why is such a law required?
   We have to ask ourselves ....

b When did this problem first arise?
   It is hard to be exact about ....

c What were the origins of this law?
   It would be useful to know ....

d How quickly can the law be implemented?
   People are asking ....

e In what areas should we implement this law?
   We have to decide ....

f What other laws will we need in the future?
   The public is asking ....

9 Conditionals (If ...)

Sentences using 'if' are called **conditionals**. They contain two parts: the 'if' clause (expressing the condition), and a 'result' clause. The 'if' clause can come first or second. If it comes first, you need a comma after it:

If you are self-employed, submitting a tax return is a legal requirement.
Submitting a tax return is a legal requirement **if you are self-employed**.

 Writing Tip

Conditional sentences are an effective way of linking causes with effects, both real and speculative.

'Real' conditionals

- The **'zero'** conditional has a present tense in both clauses and refers to the present:
  If you **work** at a computer screen all day, it **is** important to take regular breaks.

  NOTE: 'if' can often be replaced by 'when'.

- The **'first'** conditional has a present tense in the 'if' clause and a future tense in the result clause, and refers to the future:
  If Bygress plc **cuts** its costs, it **will survive** the recession.

  Provided that/**as long as** can replace *if* when the meaning is 'only if' or 'on condition that':
  Provided that/**As long as** demand **outstrips** supply, the price **will** continue to rise.

  Unless, used with a positive verb, can replace 'if' to mean 'except if' or 'if ... not':
  Customers **will** complain **unless** the service **is improved**. (NOT 'is not improved')

'Speculative' conditionals

- The **'second'** conditional has a past tense in the 'if' clause and **would** + **verb** in the result clause, and describes an action or a situation that doesn't currently exist, with the likely outcome if it did:
  If more companies **moved** their headquarters out of London, this **would benefit** regional economies.

  In formal writing, **were** is preferred in the 'if' clause to the singular form 'was':
  If fast broadband access **were** available on the island, it **would** help local businesses.

- The **'third'** conditional has a past perfect tense in the 'if' clause and **would have** + **past participle** in the result clause, and describes an action that didn't happen, with the likely outcome if it had:
  If the share price **had fallen** further, there **would have been** a takeover bid.

  In formal writing, '**Had**' may be placed at the beginning of a clause, and 'if' removed:
  Had the Government intervened, the shipyard would have remained open.

 Danger Zone

Using 'will'/'would'/'would have' in the 'if' clause

Don't use 'will'/'would'/'would have' in the 'if' clause:
There will be few winners if interest rates ~~will~~ **rise** dramatically.
If Lyot Brothers ~~would have~~ **had** sold some of their assets, they would have avoided making staff redundant.

Variations in conditional sentences

- 'Will'/'would' may be replaced by **may/might/could/can** to make the outcome less certain:
  If management had taken a softer negotiating line, the strike **might** not have happened.

- Typical tense patterns may vary: in the example below a third conditional 'if' clause is followed by a second conditional result clause to show a present outcome:
  If Sharon Brook **had remained** as CEO, the company **would be** in a much better position today.

- **Even if** … meaning 'Whether or not … ' may replace 'If … ':
  Even if the product had been re-branded, it would have made a loss.

- **But for/Without …, If it had not been for/Had it not been for …** (third conditional), **If it were not for …** (second conditional) + **noun phrase** can be used:
  But for the oil leak, BP would have made record profits.

- **Were to** + **infinitive** may be used in second conditionals:
  If the company **were to relocate**, it could reduce its energy costs.

Exercises

1 Rewrite the sentences using *if* and the modal verbs in brackets.

a Silframe did not lose their share of the youth market because they did not increase their prices. (*would*)
   If Silframe ....

b Koyley Ltd probably failed because they did not use internet marketing. (*might*)
   Koyley Ltd ....

c The sales team did not win new orders because they did not attend the trade fair in Barcelona. (*could*)
   The sales team ....

d The advertising campaign did not focus on young professionals, and it did not succeed. (*would*)
   If ....

e Harrtreat plc is flourishing today because it diversified five years ago. (*would*)
   If it ....

2 Complete each sentence with two words.

a .... its highly-skilled workforce, the north-east would not have attracted the new car plant.

b .... committee carried out a full investigation in 2019, it would have discovered that two substantial bribes had been paid.

c .... not been for the region's easy access to solar power, business costs would have soared.

d .... it had cut costs substantially, the company would not have avoided bankruptcy.

e .... had not been for their inflexible recruitment policy, the Dalkeith factory could have taken advantage of the market in part-time workers.

3 Correct any of the sentences that are wrong by adding or replacing a word.

a If CEO Barry Cranston were found guilty of insider trading, he would have to stand down.

b If video links were replace trade fairs, the human link between sales teams and retailers could be lost.

c If supermarkets did not sell goods other than foods, they would not be as profitable as they are.

d If there were not for Gouldnot's successful Paris branch, the company would be making a loss.

e Unless the agreement is signed, it has no validity in law.

f Provided as it continues to innovate, the company has a bright future.

10 Using adverbs

Adverbs go with verbs → changed **rapidly**
Adverbs can also go with adjectives **extremely** rapid and
other adverbs → **extremely rapidly**

 Writing Tip

Using adverbs correctly can greatly
improve your writing, particularly if you
use ones that convey your meaning
precisely.

▶ **Read this paragraph from an essay about changes in the music industry, look at the adverbs (in bold),
then read the rules.**

The music industry has **frequently** undergone major changes and it has always tried **hard** to adapt. It has
been affected **equally** by technological advances and demographic changes in its market. A structure that
worked **well** in one decade would prove not to be viable in another. For example, the domination of big
record companies came to an end **remarkably quickly** in the 1990s. Small independent companies could
now produce and market music **easily** and set-up costs for such companies were **reasonably** low. **Logically**,
this had major repercussions for the big companies.

 Rules

Forming adverbs

Most adverbs are formed by adding **-ly** to the adjective:
  clear → clearly   extreme → extremely

If the adjective ends with **-l**, add **-ly**:
  full → fully   essential → essentially   global → globally

If the adjective ends with **-y**, the adverb ends with **-ily**:
  happy → happily

If the adjective ends with **-ble**, the adverb ends with **-bly**:
  considerable → considerably   incredible → incredibly

If the adjective ends with **-ic**, the adverb ends **-ically**:
  basic → basically

The adverb form of **good** is **well**:
  a good idea → an idea that works well

For these common words, the adverb is the same as the adjective:
  fast → fast   hard → hard   late → late

- It is often possible to say the same thing using an adjective or an adverb:
  He felt under **constant pressure**./He felt **constantly under pressure**.

  NOTE: Adverbs often collocate with particular verbs.

  ▶ See **55** *collocations (1)*.

 Remember!

- Never use the adverb 'well' with the meaning 'very' in academic writing:
  Initially, the music industry was well pleased with the Government's copyright proposals. ✖

- Use more sophisticated adverbs instead of 'very', 'really' or 'a lot', in order to give your work a more
  academic style:
  At that time, record companies were ~~really~~ **remarkably** quick to adapt to changing fashions.

Adverbs for commenting

Adverbs are used in academic writing to comment on a situation or a fact. For example, they can be used:

to concede a point

Admittedly, some electronic music has been outstanding in terms of composition. (I admit that …)

to strengthen a comment

Clearly, solutions need to be found as soon as possible. (It is clear that …)
The effects of this development on the music industry were, **unsurprisingly**, enormous. (There was no surprise about this.)

to hedge

A **potentially** bigger advantage of teaching music to children is that it reduces the stress of studying. (It may well be the case that …)
Apparently, this problem was insurmountable for the producers.

to imply something may not be true

Seemingly, no one knew about the problem at the time. (This is what has been said, but it seems hard to believe.)

NOTE: A 'commenting' adverb can begin a sentence, in which case it should be followed by a comma; or it can come between commas later in a sentence.

 Danger Zone

Using an adjective when an adverb is required

An adverb 'describes' a verb – it gives information on how something is done or happens, or it describes an action. Most adverbs end **-ly**. Don't use an adjective when an adverb is required:

The situation improved tremendous and profits rose steady. ✖
The situation **improved tremendously** and profits rose **steadily**. ✔

Exercises

1 Decide whether or not the underlined words are correct, and correct those that are not.

a This was a problem that proved <u>incredible</u> difficult to solve.
b There are many other people who behave <u>similar</u> in these circumstances.
c The idea became <u>extraordinarily</u> popular within a short space of time.
d Attitudes to this issue have undergone <u>drastic</u> changes in recent years.
e People made a <u>desperately</u> attempt to avoid the oncoming disaster.
f People in the audience were <u>well</u> quiet during the performance.

2 Rewrite these sentences, replacing each underlined phrase with an adverb.

a <u>It was astonishing that</u> nobody had noticed this problem before.
b Similar research was going on elsewhere, <u>which was a coincidence</u>.
c <u>It was unfortunate</u> that nobody foresaw this problem.
d <u>It is obvious that</u> no firm conclusions can be drawn from so little evidence.
e Nothing could have been done to prevent the accident, <u>it appears</u>.

11 Emphasising

Emphatic language strengthens a writer's argument.

People need to appreciate that speeding causes accidents. → **What people need to appreciate is** that speeding causes accidents.

 Writing Tip

Although you often need to be cautious in academic writing, there will be other times when your tutor will expect you to express strong and confident arguments.

▶ **Read this paragraph and look at the phrases in bold, which illustrate three emphatic structures.**

Mass tourism undoubtedly brings problems as well as benefits to newly discovered regions. **Only by examining a key set of issues in detail can we decide** whether a town or region has actually benefited from tourism. A good place to start is the local economy. **What one will notice quite quickly is** the number of new businesses that have emerged since the first influx of visitors. All of these may have brought in new income and created jobs, but **it is their seasonal nature that** distinguishes them from the traditional economy: when the tourists leave, the restaurants and souvenir shops in the main tourist areas – and the streets themselves – go into a kind of hibernation, perhaps for six months on end, during which time nothing happens at all.

1 Only by + '-ing' phrase

America needs to encourage drivers to scale down the size of their cars and reduce their dependence on oil. → **Only by encouraging drivers to scale down the size of their cars will** America succeed in reducing its dependence on oil.

NOTE: This structure is normally followed by 'will' or 'can', and the word order changes.

2 What + subject + verb + be

The UK needs a Minister of Transport with a real sense of vision. → **What the UK needs is** a Minister of Transport with a real sense of vision.

3 It + is/was + noun + that/who

The tour operator should take responsibility if a hotel is overbooked. → **It is the tour operator who** should take responsibility if a hotel is overbooked.

▶ **Look at these sentences about travel and find a mistake in each one.**

It is the lack of information what makes travellers angry when there are airport delays. ✗
What are passengers looking for is a train service that is punctual and not overcrowded. ✗
Only by acting on consumer feedback travel companies can improve their performance. ✗
What's wrong: There are mistakes in the words used or in word order.

Corrected sentences

It is the lack of information **that** makes travellers angry when there are delays at airports. ✓
What passengers **are** looking for is a train service that is punctual and not overcrowded. ✓
Only by acting on consumer feedback **can** travel companies improve their performance. ✓

4 Using emphatic adverbs

Clearly, obviously, undoubtedly
Heathrow is **undoubtedly** a major success story, but it has problematic aspects.

Absolutely, completely, entirely, utterly, wholly
The travel patterns of the general public in the poorest communities of the world are **entirely** different from those in affluent countries.

Indeed
There are a number of car-sharing schemes in operation in London that are very successful **indeed**.

Quite = 'completely' when used with adjectives such as *certain, different, impossible, sure, true, wrong*
We can be **quite sure** that there will be protests against the proposed construction.

Whatsoever/at all *(added to negative statements)*
The council made no provision **at all/whatsoever** for car parking.

5 Using a word + a reflexive pronoun (*e.g. itself or themselves*)

A poorly-performing hotel can only improve if **the management itself** recognises the problems.
The use of *itself* emphasises that it is the management that needs to accept that there are problems, rather than someone else (such as the *staff*).

▶ Look back at the paragraph on page 24 and find some examples of 4 and 5.

Exercises

1 Rewrite these sentences, emphasising the important parts.

a The one-way system was making the situation worse.
It ....

b Visitors to Scotland enjoy its magnificent scenery most.
What ....

c Consumers must purchase local produce to reduce the amount of food transportation.
Only by ....

d People want easy access to the main tourist sites.
What ....

e Most passengers seek value for money rather than luxury in an airline.
It ....

f Resorts have to retain their essential character if they want to attract tourism in the long term.
Only by ....

2 Complete this text with the words below.

indeed, whatsoever, entirely, itself, undoubtedly

There is (a) .... a growing trend for independent travelling in its widest sense. This can range from travel agencies assisting customers in their tailor-made arrangements to complex trips planned with no professional input (b) .... Often it is the planning (c) .... that the new breed of traveller enjoys, and the results can prove to be very interesting (d) .... For example, a teacher from Surrey recently chose to spend a month (e) .... alone on an Indonesian island normally inhabited only by parrots and monkeys.

12   Negative words and phrases

The Minister did not offer an apology at any point.   →   **At no point** did the Minister offer an apology.

 Writing Tip

There are a number of negative words and phrases that can be very effective in academic writing. They are not commonly used in informal speech but are very appropriate in more formal contexts such as essays.

▶ In this paragraph, note the negative words and phrases in bold and the word order that follows them.

This was a particularly difficult period for the Government. **No matter** what they did, everything seemed to go wrong. **Neither** their handling of the economy at home **nor** their foreign policies abroad proved effective. **No sooner** had they weathered one storm than another arrived. **At no time** were they able to get to grips with events. Some MPs faced a dilemma: they did not want to rebel publicly against the leadership, but **neither** could they allow things to continue in this way. **Not since** the leadership battle of 20 years earlier had there been such a key moment in the party's history.

Negative phrases using the question pattern

When you use the phrases below at the beginning of a sentence, you need to place the auxiliary or modal verb (*be, have, could, will*, etc.), if there is one, or a form of *do*, in front of the subject:

Under no circumstances could the Government ~~could~~ continue their programme.
They did not want to resign, but nor ~~they had~~ **did they have** the support to carry on.

1 **No sooner ... than/hardly ... when**

   to describe one thing happening immediately or very soon after another:
   No sooner had one crisis passed than another arose.
   Hardly had one crisis passed when another arose.

2 **On no account/under no circumstances; at no time/point; in no way**

   to emphasise negative points:
   Under no circumstances/On no account could they allow their opponents to know the full facts.
   At no time did they seem to be in control of events.
   In no way could this be described as a success.

3 **Not since; not until/only when; it was not until/only when ... that**

   to refer to important points in time:
   Not since the recession 20 years earlier **had a government been** so unpopular.
   Not until/Only when the economy improved **did their popularity begin** to rise.

   NOTE: if you use **It was not until/Only when ... that**, the word order is not reversed:
   It was not until the economy improved **that their popularity began to rise**.

Neither ... nor

● These sentences say the same thing in different ways:
   The policy **did not increase** the Government's popularity, **nor did it work** in practice.
   The policy **neither increased** the Government's popularity **nor did it work** (OR **nor worked**) in practice.
   Neither did the policy increase the Government's popularity, **nor did it work** in practice.

● In these sentences, positive verbs are used:
   Neither the public **nor** their own party members **supported** the policy. (two subjects + positive verb)

The minister **neither spoke** in favour of the policy **nor criticised** it. (one subject + two different positive verbs)

No matter how/what/who, etc.

Used for saying that one fact makes no difference to another (using normal word order):
No matter how hard they tried, they could not improve the economy.
No matter what they did, they could not improve the economy.

No / no one / nothing

Use a positive verb with these negative words:
They **made no** progress for a couple of years.
The policy **pleased no one**.
They **could do nothing** right as far as the public were concerned.

Any / anyone / anything

Use these words with a negative verb:
They **did not make any** progress … The policy **did not please anyone**. They **could not do anything** right …

Exercises

1 Rewrite the sentences, starting with the words in brackets.

a As soon as people had become accustomed to the situation, it changed. (*No sooner…*)

b They worked very quickly but they could not keep up with demand. (*No matter…*)

c She got rid of one reporter but then another one appeared. (*Hardly…*)

d The policy could not be allowed to fail on any account. (*On no account…*)

e People did not begin to worry about the economy until inflation started to rise. (*It was only when…*)

f This has not been considered an important issue until recent times. (*Not until…*)

2 Decide whether or not the underlined words in these sentences are correct and correct those that are not.

a The new IT systems did not improve efficiency nor <u>were they</u> popular with staff.

b The advantages of this solution were that it would not be difficult to implement and it would not be very expensive <u>neither</u>.

c Voters listened to the politicians' words and they were neither reassured by them <u>or</u> interested in them.

d Neither the media <u>nor</u> the public accepted the official version of events.

e At the time, experts did not see <u>nothing</u> wrong with this theory.

f It was not a popular policy, nor <u>it was</u> a successful one.

13 Gerunds and infinitives

A **gerund** is a verb that ends with '**-ing**' → losing
An **infinitive** is **to** + **verb** → to improve

If we fail **to improve** distribution by December, we will risk **losing** our share of the market.

 Writing Tip

Some verbs are followed by a gerund and some by an infinitive form of another verb. (Sometimes both can be used but the form may change the meaning.)
It is important to know which form to use with verbs that are common in academic work.

▶ **Read this paragraph from an essay about industrial relations and look at the verb forms in bold.**

At the meeting, senior management and union leaders **discussed implementing** new working practices and scales of pay. They **attempted to reach** agreement on these issues and each side **expected** the other side **to compromise**. However, finding solutions to some of the areas of disagreement proved extremely difficult. **To give** everyone an opportunity to consult their colleagues, the meeting was adjourned. When the talks resumed, management **tried to make** the union leaders **see** how important it was to modernise but they remained **opposed to implementing** some of the ideas.

Verbs followed by the gerund

- Here are some examples of verbs that you might need to use in academic work that are followed by the '-ing' form of another verb:

| deny | justify | avoid/resist/delay | consider/contemplate | imagine | dislike/resent |
| suggest/recommend/discuss | | involve/mean/entail | risk | mention/describe | anticipate |

Union representatives **denied causing** the talks to break down.
The management were unable to **justify imposing** unfair terms on the workforce.
It was clear that the proposal would **entail/involve/mean making** 200 people redundant.
Union officials would not **contemplate/consider agreeing** to the terms.
Strikers **described/mentioned being** reluctant to go on strike.

Verbs followed by the infinitive

- Here are some examples of verbs that you might need to use in academic work that are followed by the infinitive form of another verb:

| threaten/demand | refuse/agree/decide/choose | claim/pretend | promise/guarantee/undertake |
| attempt | fail/manage | plan/intend/aim/mean | wish/want |

Workers **demanded to have** longer holidays and **threatened to go** on strike.
After some discussion, they **decided/chose/refused/agreed to accept** the terms.
They **claimed/pretended to represent** the views of the entire workforce.
Both sides **promised/guaranteed/undertook to honour** the agreement.

NOTE: 'Mean' followed by the gerund = 'involve'; 'mean' followed by the infinitive = 'intend'.

Verb + object + infinitive

want/expect enable/teach/allow	encourage/urge/persuade/convince/invite	warn/advise	force/drive/compel/oblige

- These verbs use this pattern:
Union leaders **encouraged/urged/persuaded/ convinced** <u>members</u> **to accept** the deal.
Militant union officials **warned/advised** <u>their colleagues</u> **not to accept** the terms.

NOTE: Force/drive/compel/oblige are usually used in the passive form:
Employees complained that they **were being forced/compelled/obliged/driven to work** unsocial hours.

 Remember!

The verbs 'make' and 'let' are followed by an infinitive without 'to':

No amount of persuasion would make the workforce to agree. ✖

No amount of persuasion would **make** the workforce **agree**. ✔

Managers should **let** the workforce **have** their say. ✔

NOTE: In the passive, 'make' is followed by 'to':

The workforce was **made to agree** to the new proposals. ✔

 Danger Zone

To + '-ing'

There are a few verbs and phrases that use the '-ing' form after 'to', not the infinitive form:
Managers were not **accustomed/used to listening** to the wishes of the workforce.
Both sides became **resigned/reconciled to compromising** on various issues.
It seemed for a while that they were **close to reaching** an agreement.
They could not **adapt/adjust to working** in those conditions.
Nobody would **admit to being** responsible for the talks breaking down.
Unable to succeed through negotiation, the leaders **resorted to making** threats.
Neither side was **looking forward to meeting** the other.

Exercises

1 Complete these sentences with the gerund, infinitive or 'to' + '-ing' form of the verbs in brackets.

a They realised that returning to profitability would mean .... (*introduce*) radical measures and they decided .... (*draft*) outline plans for this.

b They met to discuss .... (*restructure*) the department and they are now close .... (*finalise*) the details.

c If you feel that you are being obliged .... (*implement*) decisions that you don't agree with, you tend to resist .... (*carry*) them out for as long as possible.

d All department heads undertook .... (improve) productivity in their departments, but they warned management .... (not have) unrealistic expectations of what could be achieved.

e Sales figures encouraged them .... (*believe*) that their strategy was working and so they would not contemplate .... (*change*) it.

f The owners were looking forward .... (*increase*) the profits over the coming year and the consultants recommended .... (*recruit*) more staff in order to achieve this.

2 Four of the underlined verb forms in this paragraph are incorrect. Find them and correct them.

One of the major problems of his period as Prime Minister was that he could not admit <u>to make</u> any mistakes. Aides urged him <u>to do</u> so, on the grounds that it would make the public <u>to think</u> differently about him. They told him that the public expected their leaders <u>to show</u> a human side, but he refused <u>taking</u> any notice of their advice. He would not consider <u>altering</u> his approach and he denied <u>to have</u> an image that the public found off-putting. For two more years, he tried to justify <u>continuing</u> in the same old way, but eventually the voters had their say.

14   Articles: a/an, the

The grammatical term for **a/an** and **the** is **articles**.

A/an is the **indefinite article**.

The is the **definite article**.

 Writing Tip

Not using articles correctly is a basic error that will give a bad impression of your work. It is essential to use an article when it is required and it is just as essential not to use an article when it is wrong to do so.

▶ **Read this paragraph from an essay on media and look at when articles are used and not used.**

The birth of what is now commonly called **celebrity culture** can be traced to **the 1980s**. Before then, **a famous person** could assume that he or she could maintain some privacy out of **the glare of the media** and without attracting **the attention of the public**. There were **gossip columns** in **newspapers** and of course **scandals** were common, but **life** was different for celebrities until the 1980s. During that decade there was **a huge change** in **attitudes towards famous people** and this coincided with **the arrival of** new magazines such as *Hello*. **The celebrities they covered** were paid **large sums** to give **readers an insight into** their private lives, and **the stories and interviews** in the magazines took **an uncritical view** of their subjects. **The change in attitudes** started here.

Use 'a/an' ...

- to talk about one of many, but not a particular one: a famous person → any famous person

- when you are using a singular noun for the first time, not referring to someone or something already mentioned: a huge change → the word 'change' is introduced here.

 Danger Zone
Words beginning with 'h'

If 'h' is pronounced when you say the word, use 'a':
a happy society
a habitat

If 'h' is not pronounced when you say the word, use 'an':
an honest man   a honest man ✖
an hour   a hour ✖

Use 'the' ...

- when there can only be one:
the birth of/the arrival of

- when you are referring to a specific one or ones and saying which one or ones:
the glare of the media/the attention of the public/the celebrities that they covered → which glare, whose attention, which celebrities are all explained in the phrases

- before something that has been mentioned earlier:
The change in attitudes started here. → *the change previously mentioned*

- before a group noun:
the media/the public *(but not 'the society')*

  ▶ See also **3** *Singular or plural subjects and verbs*.

- Before a decade or century:
the 1980s

Don't use 'the' ...

- with plural nouns when you are generalising rather than specifying which ones:
  gossip columns in newspapers/scandals were common → *particular gossip columns, newspapers and scandals are not specified*

- with singular nouns that describe abstract concepts or ideas rather than particular examples of these:
  life was different → *this refers to the abstract concept of 'life', not a particular life*

- with plural nouns when you have not mentioned them previously:
  attitudes towards famous people/large sums → *these do not refer to any attitudes or sums previously mentioned*

- with plural nouns when it is understood which ones you are talking about:
  readers → *this can only refer to readers of the magazines being discussed*

  NOTE: All these sentences could be correctly written with 'the' if the noun were followed by a phrase explaining or specifying which one or ones were being described.

  Nowadays, people often have conversations about **the celebrities who are in the news.**
  The wealth and happiness shown in these magazines fascinates people.
  Some people say that **the articles in these magazines** are worthless.

Exercises

1 Decide whether or not these sentences are correct and correct those that are not.

a For most parents, the education is one of the biggest sources of a concern with regard to their children.
b There were huge differences between the incomes of people living in the same street.
c Despite spending the large amounts of money, the Government did not manage to achieve its targets for the health care.
d It has been argued that people now have the higher expectations of the life and that this can cause them an unhappiness.

2 Complete these sentences with the correct article or no article.

a In 1955, he travelled to India and, on his return, he wrote .... emotional account of .... experiences he had had on .... journey.
b Towards .... end of .... 20th century, ... lives of many people in .... developed countries were transformed by .... arrival of .... computer technology.
c Suddenly, ... entire industry changed and .... new approach was required to .... whole area of marketing.
d There wasn't .... obvious solution to .... problem and .... opinions varied as to .... best course of action.
e Many people claim in .... surveys that .... job satisfaction is more important than .... high salary.

15 Relative clauses: who, which, that, etc.

Brunel was the engineer who first realised the potential of wider tracks for higher-speed trains.

The clause in bold above is called a **relative clause**, and the word 'who' is a **relative pronoun**.

 Writing Tip

Relative clauses allow you to define and add information to what you are saying. Used correctly, they can be a very effective writing tool.

 Rules

There are two types of relative clause:

1 **Defining relative clauses**, where the information in the clause is essential to the sentence:
   The integrated circuit was the key development **that led to the personal computer**.
   The patients **who had listened to music before surgery** seemed to have experienced less pain.
   Without the relative clause, these sentences lose their meaning.
   In defining clauses, 'that' may be used instead of 'which', 'who' and 'whom'

2 **Non-defining relative clauses**, where the information in the clause is useful, but additional:
   Optical fibres, **which have a much higher capacity than copper cables**, have revolutionised the telecommunications industry.
   Without the relative clause, the sentence still conveys its basic meaning.
   In non-defining clauses you may not replace 'which', 'who' or 'whom' with 'that', and the clause itself must be separated from the rest of the sentence by commas.

▶ **Decide what's wrong with the sentences on the left, before looking at the explanations on the right.**

A patent is a legal document, which prevents others from exploiting an invention for a fixed period. ✖

→ *The information about a patent is essential to the sentence, so there should not be a comma, and 'that' is preferable to 'which'.*

Grace Hopper who was born in 1906 in New York developed the idea of computer languages. ✖

→ *The information about Hopper's birth is not essential so the relative clause 'who … New York' needs to be enclosed by commas.*

In 2006, Pluto was reclassified as a 'dwarf planet' by the International Astronomical Union, that is a recognised body of professional astronomers. ✖

→ *This is an example of the second type of relative clause, so 'which' cannot become 'that'.*

Corrected sentences

A patent is a legal document that prevents others from exploiting an invention for a fixed period. ✔

Grace Hopper, who was born in 1906 in New York, developed the idea of computer languages. ✔

In 2006, Pluto was reclassified as a 'dwarf planet' by the International Astronomical Union, which is a recognised body of professional astronomers. ✔

 Remember!

In a relative clause, *which* can sometimes refer to a whole 'idea':

The geneticist discussed his hope of finding a cure for Alzheimer's, **which** inspired many in his audience.
Here 'which' = 'his hope of finding a cure for Alzheimer's'.

Improve Your Grammar

Who and whom

- whom is normally used in formal writing when it is the object of the clause, and **always after prepositions** such as *by, for, from, to, with*, etc.
  The enquiry was led by Gregory Stillman, **whom** the government appointed in 2020. (The government appointed him.)
  Stephen Hawking is the physicist **with** ~~who~~ **whom** the general public is most familiar.
  NOTE: 'whom' is not simply a more sophisticated form of 'who' and cannot be used generally instead of 'who'.

Whose and which

whose + **noun** shows 'possession' for people and things
The Anti-Vivisection League is an organisation **whose opposition** to experiments on animals is well known.
whose → the Anti-Vivisection League's
NOTE: Do not confuse **whose** and **who's** (= who is).

of which used when writing about things
A European conference on embryo research, **whose details/the details of which** have not yet been announced, is likely to be held in Milan next year.

way in which and **extent to which**
The way in which engineering is perceived by young people may have to change before we see an increase in its popularity as a university subject.

where instead of **in which** with the words *place, area, situation*, etc.
The treatment of anexoria nervosa and bulimia is an area **in which/where** there is a great deal of disagreement.

Exercises

1 Decide whether or not these sentences are correct, and correct those that are not.

  a Much research has been conducted into schizophrenia, that causes chronic behavioural problems.
  b Cox argues that it was the Universal Turing Machine of the 1930s that led the way to digital computing.
  c Newton and Einstein are considered to be the scientists to who modern physics owes the greatest debt.
  d Water which may indicate the presence of life may have existed relatively recently on the surface of Mars.
  e Dr Abel chairs a panel whose views on stem-cell research are regularly reported in the media.

2 Rewrite these sentences to include the information in brackets.

  a A number of questions were asked about the equipment. (*It was used in the experiment.*)
  b The Jodrell Bank Observatory has played an important part in researching meteors, pulsars and quasars. (*It was established in 1945.*)
  c John Nash made some of the key early insights into modern game theory. (*This led to his being co-awarded the Nobel Prize in 1994.*)
  d Michael Faraday was a scientist. (*His research into magnetic fields gained him his reputation.*)
  e The audience were introduced to Margaret Simons. (*She had first identified two of the species of spider being discussed.*)

3 Fill each gap in these texts with a preposition + 'which', 'whose' or 'whom'.

  a The engineer and entrepreneur James Dyson has been critical of the UK business environment for the way .... it has prioritised selling and marketing over design and manufacturing.
  b Scientists are the people .... we turn for the cures for all our illnesses, yet many complain about the extent .... research funding ignores lesser-known diseases.
  c Louis Pasteur is the French chemist .... the process of 'pasteurisation' is named.

16 Comparing and contrasting

Adjective: good; **comparative adjective**: better; **superlative adjective**: best/worst.
Adverb: efficiently; **comparative adverb**: more efficiently; **superlative adverb**: most efficiently.

 Rules

- Add -er/-est to **one-syllable** adjectives (adj.) and adverbs (adv.):
  (adj.) low → lower → lowest; (adv.) soon → sooner → soonest;
  but 'double' the consonant when there is a single vowel + a single consonant:
  big → bigger → biggest; hot → hotter → hottest.

- Add -er/-est to **two-syllable** adjectives ending in -ow, -er (and -y, but change the -y to -i):
  narrow → narrower → narrowest; clever → cleverer → cleverest; noisy → noisier → noisiest.

- Use more/most or less/least with adverbs and all other adjectives of **two syllables or more**:
  (adv.) efficiently → more/less efficiently → most/least efficiently;
  (adj.) famous → more/less famous → most/least famous.

- Note the exceptions:
  (adj.) good/(adv.) well → better → best; (adj.) bad/(adv.) badly → worse → worst;
  far → further → furthest (farther/farthest is also possible, but less common).

Two main structures

1 Comparative adjective/adverb + than

Manufacturing costs are **higher** in southern China **than** in the poorer inland regions.
For the third successive year, Fall Tor plc is trading **less successfully than** its competitors.

2 (Not) as + adjective/adverb + as

Research shows that start-up companies in the manufacturing sector are **not** performing **as well as** new businesses in the service sector.

Note where 'a' or 'an' is placed in the phrase 'as' + adjective + noun:
Despite a poor first quarter, 2018 was **not as** difficult **a** year for most SMEs **as** 2019.

 Danger Zone

NOT 'more easier'
If '-er' has been added to an adjective, it is wrong to use 'more' as well. If 'more' is being used with an adverb, the adverb should have the normal ending.

Manufacturing products can be ~~more~~ **easier than** selling them. ✔
The manufacturing team met their deadlines **more** ~~easier~~ **easily than** they had expected. ✔

less/fewer
Remember to use 'fewer' with plural words.

fewer customers ✔
less money ✔
We have ~~less~~ **fewer** customers on Sunday than on Saturday. ✔

▶ Decide what's wrong with the sentences on the left before looking at the corrected sentences on the right.

In 2018, SWTU Ltd produced a new mobile phone that was more thin than its existing models. ✖	→	In 2018, SWTU Ltd produced a new mobile phone that was **thinner** than its existing models. ✔
Land was cheap, but skilled labour was not as easy to find by the coast than in the cities. ✖	→	Land was cheap, but skilled labour was not as easy to find by the coast **as** in the cities. ✔
The company realised that coal supplies could be delivered more cheap by road than by rail. ✖	→	The company realised that coal supplies could be delivered more **cheaply** by road than by rail. ✔
The worse year for the factory in terms of production was 2016, when there were two strikes. ✖	→	The **worst** year for the factory in terms of production was 2016, when there were two strikes. ✔

 Remember!

You can make comparisons with expectations, or with the past.

Finding a new location for the factory was **more difficult** than the management team had predicted.
The construction of smaller flats, often for the buy-to-let market, is **not as profitable as** it was ten years ago.

Exercises

1 Rewrite the sentences using the word(s) in brackets and beginning with the underlined words.

a Staff development opportunities are not as important to factory employees as clear lines of communication. (*less … than*)
b Raw materials cannot be transported as quickly by road as by train. (*more … than*)
c British businesses are spending less than European companies on product design, according to recent studies. (*not … as … as*)
d The replacements from Germany were not as heavy as the French engines. (*… than*)
e Export results and import figures are equally impressive this year. (*as … as*)
f The safety systems were not checked as frequently as they should have been. (*less … than*)

2 Decide which of these sentences are correct, and correct those that are not.

a Kellsver was asked to design a vehicle that would operate in the wetest conditions.
b It was not as effective system as the manufacturers had hoped.
c Smails plc realised that its profit margins would be slimmer in the UK than abroad.
d Generally speaking, there are less opportunities for apprenticeships these days.
e If the parts are cooled by water, the process can be completed more sooner.
f GBTY plc's factory in Berwick is the furthest from London.
g Some of the world's most desirable cars are criticised for also being the less fuel-efficient.
h The workforce agreed that a shift system was the most safe way of working.

The cave in the rocks turned out to be **at least four times bigger** than geologists had expected.

Writing Tip

Academic writing needs to be clear and precise. You can use a whole range of words and expressions to achieve this – rather than simply saying, for example, that something is 'bigger' than something else.

▶ Read this paragraph on river pollution, noting the words and phrases that are used to describe similarities and differences.

> Although the Danube is **more than twice as long as** the Rhine, **both are similar in that** they have their sources in central Europe. The Danube, however, **unlike** the westward-flowing Rhine, travels east through countries that have not been able to invest in expensive water-treatment plants. While the Rhine Action Programme has ensured that the river is **80 per cent cleaner** than it was 20 years ago, the Danube Pollution Reduction Programme, **in contrast**, has been far less successful.

Modifying adjectives and adverbs

- For structures with a comparative adjective or adverb (+ *than*), you can use *much, a great deal, far,* or the opposites *slightly, a little, marginally* – or percentages (as in the text above):
  Earthquake damage is **much greater** in areas where housing has been poorly constructed.
  The tornado that struck New York was **marginally less powerful** than predicted.

- For structures with as (*... as*), you can use *just, almost, nearly, not quite* or *not nearly*:
  Boulders are **just as effective as** seawalls in preventing erosion, and **not nearly** as expensive.

- For superlatives, you can use *almost, one/some of* or the opposite *by far*:
  Vindija is a cave in Croatia that contains **some of the best** preserved Neanderthal remains in the world.

Numbers

For numbers, use *twice + as (many) ... as* or *three/four times + as (many) ... as* or *than* – and you can be even more precise by adding *at least, nearly, more than* or *exactly*:
In Ireland, there are **nearly twice as many** sheep as people.
Fertile soil is being lost in Europe **more than 50 times faster** than natural processes can replace it.

Words and phrases for similarity

Alike, similar to, like, to resemble
Leopards and panthers are **alike/similar in that** both of these big cats are strong swimmers.
Lake Huron **is similar to/is like/resembles** Lake Michigan **in terms of/as regards/with respect to** surface area and maximum depth.

In the same way, similarly
Ecologists have argued that heavy logging is destroying large tracts of the Amazon Rainforest. **In the same way/Similarly**, urban clearance is reducing West Africa's rainforest.

Similarity, in common
The main **similarity between** America and Australia is the large coastal population.
All cultivated crops **have** several characteristics **in common/have several similarities**.

Words and phrases for contrast

Dissimilar to, different from, unlike, to differ

The Grey Whale **is dissimilar to/is different from/differs from/is unlike** other baleen whales **in that** it feeds by filtering small organisms from the mud of shallow seas.

In contrast to, contrary to, unlike

'Flying squirrels', **in contrast to/contrary to/unlike** bats, glide rather than actually fly.

 **Danger Zone**

On the contrary, in contrast, on the other hand

On the contrary means that the opposite is true, but *in contrast* and *on the other hand* link two contrasting but equally true situations:

The future of the koala is by no means secure. **On the contrary**, habitat loss and urbanisation may well require the Australian Government to designate these mammals as a 'threatened' species. ✔

A tornado 'watch alert' tells the public that the conditions that cause tornados are present. A 'warning alert', **on the other hand/in contrast**, is issued when an eyewitness has actually made a sighting. ✔

Coastal erosion has not worsened over the past decade. *On the other hand*, coastlines have remained intact. ✘

Exercises

1 Choose the correct word or phrase from the brackets to complete each sentence.

a A new study of the state of the world's biodiversity suggests that species are dying out .... (*by far/twice as/far*) faster than scientists had previously thought.

b On account of their moveable thumbs, chimpanzees are .... (*just/exactly/slightly*) as able as humans to grasp and hold on to objects.

c Studies show that Antarctic ice is melting .... (*more/twice as/by far*) quickly as ten years ago.

d The kori bustard is .... (*one of/far/at least*) the heaviest birds in the world capable of flight.

e According to UK Kennel Club registrations, the Labrador Retriever is .... (*at least/by far/slightly*) four times more popular than the King Charles Spaniel.

2 Complete the sentences by putting a word or phrase from the box in each space.

differ	in common	similarly	in contrast	on the contrary

a The survival of these villages depends on the stock of local tuna. ...., secondary industries nearby, such as canning, rely on regular supplies of this fish.

b Summers on the coast .... from the tropical inland area in that they are windy and cool.

c Discoveries of shale gas are not met with universal approval; ...., many commentators fear the environmental damage that extraction will bring.

d The soil in these two regions has a number of features ....

e .... to Brown's study, Fisher notes a decline in the numbers of wildflowers.

18 Using noun phrases

systems → a noun

traffic-calming systems → a noun phrase

 Writing Tip

Building sentences around nouns rather than verbs or adjectives is a typical feature of academic English, and helps to create its impersonal style.

▶ Compare these two sentences on the subject of local politics.

If community groups <u>get together to buy</u> land, they can, in some cases, <u>prevent</u> it from <u>being developed</u>.	→	This sentence is built around the underlined verbs.
The joint purchase of land by community groups enables them, in some cases, to prevent **development**.	→	This sentence is built around a noun phrase and a noun (both in bold).

Creating sentences based on nouns

1 Using the noun form of verbs or adjectives

Councillors criticised the way in which newspapers <u>covered</u> the local elections.
Councillors criticised **newspaper coverage of** the local elections.
Several councillors wondered how <u>reliable</u> the traffic statistics were.
Several councillors questioned **the reliability of** the traffic statistics.

 Remember!

Using nouns and noun phrases makes it possible to put the important idea (e.g. *the joint purchase of land*) at the front of the sentence.

2 Using a noun with the same meaning as a whole phrase

A number of people doubted that the recycling scheme <u>could be kept going for a long time</u>.
There were doubts about **the sustainability of** the recycling scheme.
Local residents opposed the way in which the council <u>put</u> the new planning laws <u>into practice</u>.
There was local opposition to the council's **implementation of** the new planning laws.

3 Using the '-ing' form of a verb as a noun

If the town hall's facade were <u>cleaned</u>, it could become a more attractive local feature.
The cleaning of the town hall's facade could make it a more attractive local feature.

Nouns with compound adjectives

- A compound adjective consists of two words, usually with a hyphen between them.

- Compound adjectives are often used instead of relative clauses.
  ◗ see **15** *Relative clauses.*

<u>Services that are run by the council</u> were suspended during the strike of workers in the public sector, which lasted three days.	→	**Council-run services** were suspended during the **three-day**, **public-sector strike**.
<u>The art gallery, which had been newly restored</u>, was reopened by the Mayor.	→	**The newly-restored art gallery** was reopened by the Mayor.

Nouns with 'that ...' clauses

- A noun can be followed by a 'that ... ' clause to form the subject of a verb:
  The proposition that a bypass would solve the town's traffic problems was not accepted locally.
  Here, the bold part of the sentence forms the subject of the verb 'was not accepted'.

- A noun + 'that ... ' clause can also come in the middle or at the end of a sentence:
  House prices fell when **the news that a bypass might be built** was released.
  Local protest groups refused to accept **the view that the new road would reduce city-centre traffic**.

- The following nouns are all commonly used with 'that ... ' clauses:

idea, hypothesis, view, proposition likelihood, possibility, probability	statement, news, warning assumption, belief, claim	fact, rule, conclusion danger, risk

 Remember!

In a **noun + 'that ... ' clause**, the word *that* should not be left out.

The belief the situation was deteriorating was widespread among local residents. ✖
The belief that the situation was deteriorating was widespread among local residents. ✔

Exercises

1 Complete the sentences with a noun phrase or a compound adjective.

a The council has decided to construct a one-way system to reduce city-centre traffic.
The .... a one-way system will allow the council to reduce city-centre traffic.
b The chairperson questioned whether some of the research was relevant.
The chairperson questioned the .... some of the research.
c The town's provision of cheaper housing has been getting better in recent years.
There have been .... the town's provision of cheaper housing in recent years.
d The arena, which has been adapted specially, will host the athletics contest.
The .... arena will host the athletics contest.
e House prices have risen in the suburbs, which are expanding rapidly.
House prices have risen in the .... suburbs.

2 Rewrite the sentences, replacing the underlined part with a noun phrase or compound adjective.

a Because <u>it was likely</u> that residents would object, the proposal was withdrawn.
b The council made final changes to the celebrations, <u>which had been carefully planned</u>.
c Local councillors understood <u>how important</u> the theatre was to the town.
d The view, <u>which many people held</u>, was that the council had acted too slowly.

19 Commas (1): correct uses

 Writing Tip
Commas provide more than just pauses in your writing. There are rules for their use, and they can be vital to the meaning of a sentence.

Commas separating clauses

Clauses with participles
Relations between the two countries became strained, **leading** to open hostility.
The talks **having broken down**, relations between the two countries became even more strained.
▶ See **34** *Participles*.

Non-defining relative clauses (which give additional information)
There was disagreement on a number of foreign-policy issues, **which** caused relations between the two countries to become strained.
▶ See **15** *Relative clauses*.

Clauses with linking words and phrases
Despite attempts to repair relations between the two countries, hostilities were resumed.

Clauses within clauses
Use commas before and after a clause that comes within a clause:
Relations between the two countries, **which had not been cordial for some time**, deteriorated into open hostility.
The problem, **caused by a number of factors**, badly affected relations between them.

Sentences with more than two clauses
- If one complete clause follows another, separate them with a comma:
Caused by a number of factors, the problem badly affected relations, which had previously been cordial.

- Put commas before and after a clause within a clause, and separate any other clauses with commas also:
Relations between the two countries, **which had not been cordial for some time**, deteriorated into open hostility, **and** this situation lasted for over a decade.
  ▶ See **2** *Parts of a sentence*.

Commas separating words and phrases

- Before a **quotation**:
The statement began, 'After many hours of talks, we have been unable to reach agreement.'

  NOTE: You can also use a colon instead of a comma to introduce a quotation.
  ▶ See **24** *Inverted commas*.

- With **references**, for example to give the name of someone or the title of something previously mentioned:
The Prime Minister at that time, Edward Heath, supported a peace formula in Northern Ireland.
The proposed agreement, the Sunningdale Agreement, was discussed at that meeting.

- When giving **extra, relevant information** about something or someone previously mentioned:
  There was widespread rioting in the Falls Road, an area of Belfast.

- Separating **items in a list**:
  The issues surrounding 'The Troubles' in Northern Ireland included sectarian violence, the idea of power-sharing, the province's relations with the rest of the United Kingdom(,) and terrorism on the mainland.

  NOTE: A comma is not essential if the last item in a list is preceded by 'and' or 'or'.
  ◗ See 'Punctuating lists' in **21** *Colons and semicolons.*

- With linkers: **however, nevertheless, therefore, consequently, in addition, instead, as a result, on the other hand, furthermore, moreover**

  Use a comma after these words if they begin a sentence:
  The talks were aimed at improving relations. **Instead**, they caused them to deteriorate.

  Use a comma before and after these words if they do not begin a sentence:
  The talks, **therefore**, did not achieve their aim of improving relations.
  ◗ See **26, 27, 28** and **29** *Linking.*

- With **adverbs used instead of a clause**:
  Attempts were made to find a solution. These attempts, unfortunately, were unsuccessful./Unfortunately, these attempts were unsuccessful.
  ◗ See **49** *Using adverbs.*

- With these words and phrases: **of course, for example, namely**:
  This incident, of course, led to retaliation.
  There were numerous bombings in mainland Britain, for example, in a pub in Birmingham. A new organisation was formed, namely the Provisional IRA.

- Before a **town/city, state/county or country** if you are referring to a place in it:
  Princeton, New Jersey
  King's College, London

- Between **adjectives** when more than one is used, particularly if they are similar in meaning:
  The Troubles in Northern Ireland were long, complex and painful.

  NOTE: Use 'and' before the last adjective but not between any of the others.

 Remember!
Read back every sentence you have written to make sure that you have put in commas where they are essential.

Exercise

1 Insert any necessary commas in this paragraph.

On 20 July 1969 having stepped onto the Moon's surface Neil Armstrong uttered the famous words 'One small step for man one giant leap for mankind.' Although it had been hoped that the Moon landing would lead to significant advances in space travel some of which may soon become a reality scientific progress has generally been slow. However space research has done much to unite nations. The establishment of the International Space Station the Space Shuttle and the Hubble Telescope illustrates how much easier and more profitable it is for nations to work as a team rather than in isolation.

20   Commas (2): incorrect uses

 Writing Tip

Even if the rest of your sentence is perfectly good, adding commas where they should not be used will automatically lower the standard of your work.

 Remember!

Read back every sentence you have written to make sure that any commas you have put in really should be there.

Never use a comma ...

with a clause beginning 'that ...':
The exam results <u>indicated, that</u> children were improving at maths and science. ✗
The Department of Education <u>announced, that</u> there would be reforms to the system. ✗

between a subject and its verb:
<u>Teachers with many years of experience, were</u> beginning to leave the profession. ✗

between two subjects linked by 'and':
<u>The professor, and his colleagues</u> carried out important research into primary education in the UK. ✗

in a phrase involving a group of words that belong together as a single unit, for example:

between a noun or an adjective and a preposition that goes with it:
There was <u>a considerable improvement, in</u> the performance of boys in that age group. ✗

between a verb and a word or phrase that goes with it:
Pupils were given the opportunity to <u>vote, for</u> members of their own council. ✗

before 'or' if it comes between two adjectives, nouns or verbs:
Pupils covered this subject <u>in the second, or third year</u> of their course. ✗

▶ Decide what's wrong with the sentences on the left, before looking at the explanations on the right.

Professor Granger, and his team presented the results of their research. ✗   →   No comma between two subjects linked by 'and'

Children, whose parents went to university were also likely to go on to higher education. ✗   →   No comma before a defining relative clause

Sociologists argue, that streaming motivates the most able students. ✗   →   No comma before a clause beginning 'that'

Pupils were allowed to write, or type their answers. ✗   →   No comma before 'or' when it comes between two verbs

Course dates for some subjects, have changed. ✗   →   No comma between a subject and its verb

Danger Zone

Comma 'splicing'

This term means incorrectly using a comma between what should be two complete sentences, e.g.:

Graphic design can be seen in many places in modern life, it extends well beyond the world of advertising. ✖

This is an incorrect sentence. It could be correctly written:

as two sentences, with a full stop and a capital letter:

Graphic design can be seen in many places in modern life. It extends well beyond the world of advertising. ✔

using a linking word or phrase to form one correct sentence:

Graphic design can be seen in many places in modern life(,) and it extends well beyond the world of advertising. ✔

by linking the two sentences with a semicolon:

Graphic design can be seen in many places in modern life; it extends well beyond the world of advertising. ✔

▶ See **21** *Colons and semicolons.*

Exercises

1 Correct these sentences by adding commas, where appropriate.

a As part of the course you will analyse the theoretical ideas of socialism conservatism and liberalism.

b The Education Authority realising that primary and secondary schools in some areas had too many applicants devised a new admissions policy.

c As the education plan proved to be flawed impractical and unprofitable it was quickly abandoned.

d The Government has announced that students who live in rented accommodation are ineligible for financial assistance whatever their circumstances.

e 'Labelling' the act of saying that a child is of a certain type usually works to the child's disadvantage.

2 Insert commas in this paragraph, where they are appropriate.

According to this week's media in particular the mainstream newspapers class sizes in some British schools in the City of London are too big for Head Teachers to cope with and as a consequence some children are not fulfilling their academic potential. As a result of pressure from professionals in education the Mayor has ordered an official enquiry into the situation which will be run by Generating Genius a charitable organisation that has already helped some teenagers from poorer socioeconomic backgrounds to get good university places. The enquiry which will take place over the next ten months will look into a range of educational issues including overcrowding in classrooms improving overall standards and promoting relationships between state and independent schools. On 12th November the Mayor will speak at the Institute of Education where in the words of one reporter 'there will be considerable interest in what he has to say'. In the meantime in order to ensure that class sizes do not get out of hand it is possible that the Greater London Authority will take steps to alleviate the situation by for example allocating some of its own buildings to the education of its city's young people.

21 Colons and semicolons

 Writing Tip

Some people avoid using colons (:) and semicolons (;) because they are not sure how to use them correctly or appropriately. However, these punctuation marks are useful and important features of academic writing.

Colons

▶ **Read these sentences from a social studies essay and find the punctuation errors, then look at the correct sentences and rules below.**

A government report highlighted three main causes of crime in the inner city. High unemployment, poor housing and family breakdown. ✖

The report concluded as follows. 'Solving the problems of the inner city is not simply a question of providing money for initiatives.' ✖

The report raised one serious question, how could these problems best be addressed to improve quality of life for those in the inner city? ✖

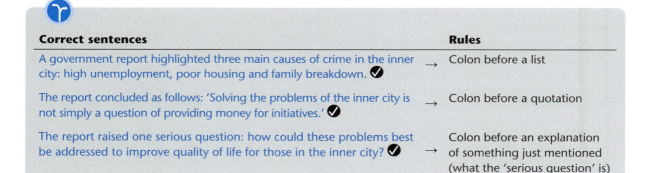

Correct sentences		Rules
A government report highlighted three main causes of crime in the inner city: high unemployment, poor housing and family breakdown. ✔	→	Colon before a list
The report concluded as follows: 'Solving the problems of the inner city is not simply a question of providing money for initiatives.' ✔	→	Colon before a quotation
The report raised one serious question: how could these problems best be addressed to improve quality of life for those in the inner city? ✔	→	Colon before an explanation of something just mentioned (what the 'serious question' is)

 Remember!

Do not use a colon when reporting someone's words with 'that'.

There are experts who say that: housing is the most important inner-city issue. ✖

Semicolons

▶ **Now think about how semicolons can be used in these sentences from the same essay.**

A government report highlighted three main causes of crime in the inner city: there had been a considerable recent rise in unemployment and a significant number of people were living in poor housing conditions and family breakdown was a major factor in levels of youth crime. ✖

The report concluded that solving the problems of the inner city was not simply a question of providing money for initiatives, any such solutions would also require a major change in attitudes. ✖

Sentences with semicolons inserted		Rules
A government report highlighted three main causes of crime in the inner city: there had been a considerable recent rise in unemployment; a significant number of people were living in poor housing conditions; and family breakdown was a major factor in levels of youth crime. ✓	→	Semicolon between long phrases or sentences in a list
The report concluded that solving the problems of the inner city was not simply a question of providing money for initiatives; any such solutions would also require a major change in attitudes. ✓	→	Semicolon to separate two complete sentences where the second one continues a point made in the first

 Remember!

Do not use semicolons where a comma is required.

Despite the construction of a ring-road; traffic congestion worsened. ✗
Despite the construction of a ring-road, traffic congestion worsened. ✓

"Don't forget about us!"

① Danger Zone
Punctuating lists

Use colons and semicolons to make lists of long phrases clear.

In the survey, people living in rural areas reported that their major concerns were as follows: lack of regular public transport services; the need to make car journeys to shop in retail parks; rising property prices due to homes being bought by wealthy outsiders; and the loss of jobs in agricultural and related industries. ✓

The colon introduces the list and the semicolons separate the items in the list.

Exercises

1 Insert colons and/or semicolons in the sentences.

a The report focuses on three issues how reliable public transport systems are what measures would be most effective in reducing traffic congestion and whether parking facilities are adequate.

b Most reports on the inner city focus on problems in fact there have been many improvements too.

c This leads us to an important development in town planning the arrival of out-of-town shopping centres.

d Tomlinson was correct when he made the statement 'Urban planners should always aim to avoid demolishing historic buildings.'

e Among town planners today, there is one buzzword sustainability.

2 Find the punctuation mistakes in these sentences and correct them.

a This brings me to my final point; the repercussions of these initiatives have not been fully considered.

b The drive to create a sustainable environment raises a serious question, to what extent should function take precedence over form?

c People who argue that: cities are becoming overcrowded should ask themselves why.

d In some societies, homes need to be built to accommodate a range of family structures, including extended families; nuclear families; and single-parent households.

22 Hyphens, dashes and brackets

A **hyphen** (-) has no space before or after it: semi-detached.
A **dash** (–) has a space both before and after it: It worked – but only for a short time.
Brackets ( ) must come in pairs: (in other words, one at the beginning and one at the end).

 Writing Tip
Hyphens are not used these days as much as they used to be, but there are certain times when you should use one. Brackets and dashes can be used effectively in academic work to separate information in sentences.

Using hyphens

- between parts of an **adjective** formed from **two or more complete words**:
  middle-aged   user-friendly   customer-driven

- after certain prefixes: e.g. **semi-, ex-, counter-, e-, self-**:
  semi-detached   ex-colleague   counter-productive   e-commerce   self-conscious
  with **co-** if referring to people: co-author   co-founder
  NOTE: Over time, hyphens have been dropped from some words, such as semicircle and countermeasure.

- for words consisting of **a number and another word**: a three-stage process

- for an **age** used as an adjective: a 40-year-old man BUT *40 years old*

- in phrases beginning **well** and with certain other phrases, only if they are used **before a noun**:
  state-of-the-art equipment   up-to-date information   well-planned courses   long-term solutions
  BUT: *The equipment is state of the art./Keep up to date with all the latest information. etc.*

Using dashes

- at the end of a sentence to **add a thought or comment** on what has just been said:
  Strict dietary guidelines for the playing squad transformed their fitness levels – to an astonishing degree.

 Remember!
Don't overuse dashes. Doing so might make your work look too informal in style.

- at the end of a sentence to **summarise or conclude** what has gone before:
  Team morale, performance in matches and the response of fans were all transformed by this new mental approach among the players – in short, it improved everything.
  NOTE: You could use a semicolon instead of the dash here.

Using brackets

- for **cross-references**: This is important with regard to fitness conditioning (see also Section 3).

- for **sources of information**, such as authors, researchers, books, reports, etc.
  One study found that fitness was 'not the major factor in successful performance' (Gregory, 2004).

- around **numbers or letters** for separate points in a sentence:
  They won, not because they were the better team but because (a) they had prepared better than their opponents and (b) they were more focused during the game.
  NOTE: You should not do this for more than two or at most three points. For a longer list, use semicolons.

- at the **end** of a sentence to **add information that is not essential**:
  Results improved a great deal (though there were occasional defeats).

- for a **whole sentence** that adds **extra but not essential** information:
  All of these studies indicated that diet and lifestyle were as important as skill and fitness with regard to differences in results for the very top players. (This was not the case for average players, but our focus here is on top players.)
  NOTE: The full stop that ends the full sentence must come before the second bracket.

Remember!

If you plan to use a pair of dashes or brackets, check that you have included the second one.

Using dashes or brackets

- in the **middle** of a sentence to **add information that is not essential** but may be useful or interesting:
  Strict dietary guidelines – a recent innovation at that time – transformed the athletes' fitness.
  Strict dietary guidelines (a recent innovation at that time) transformed the athletes' fitness.
  NOTE: Commas could also be used here instead of dashes or brackets.

- to **explain** something that has just been mentioned in a sentence:
  The practice of visualising – imagining yourself at key points during a game – proved to be very helpful.
  The practice of visualising (imagining yourself at key points during a game) proved to be very helpful.

Exercises

1 Add hyphens where they are required.

a This was a well received reform at the time. Prior to that change, only upper class people had been able to vote.
b The records were not up to date and an old fashioned system was still in place.
c His codefendant in the case was his former boss, and after a three month trial they were both found guilty.
d By the time he was thirty years old, he had a high powered job advising the Government on state run services.
e Countries wanted self determination and the status of being fully independent.

2 Use dashes where they are appropriate.

a Opponents questioned the logic of his argument much to his annoyance.
b He made a speech in the House of Commons and this was not the only time when he went against his own party in which he heavily criticised the policy.
c Mistakes were made, inefficiency dogged the entire project, and complaints came in from all sides, this was not how things were supposed to be.
d Pensioners regardless of their personal and financial circumstances were all better off because of this change.

3 Use brackets where they are appropriate.

a There were exceptions to this pattern but the results were generally very consistent. Exceptions are listed in the table below. It was therefore possible to draw firm conclusions.
b He was a strong supporter of entry into the Eurozone and played a significant role in the country's decision to take that step. He later regretted this, but that was far in the future.
c In her influential report *Approaches to Poverty*, 2020, Browne proposed wholesale changes to welfare rules.
d The unforeseen consequence fewer workers having job security seriously affected morale in the industry.

23 Apostrophes

 Writing Tip

Despite the misuse and omission of apostrophes in some forms of everyday English, they are an important feature of academic writing and distinguish a 'sloppy' writer from a careful one.

▶ **Read these sentences on the subject of US history and find the punctuation errors.**

It could be argued that Kennedys assassination contributed to the upheaval that took place in the 1960's in the US. ✖

The Vietnam War and it's repercussions had a profound influence on US society and its a subject that still arouses strong feelings. ✖

What's wrong: There is one missing apostrophe and one apostrophe that should not be there in each sentence. The sentences should read:

It could be argued that **Kennedy's** assassination contributed to the upheaval that took place in the **1960s** in the US. ✔

The Vietnam War and **its** repercussions had a profound influence on US society and **it's** a subject that still arouses strong feelings. ✔

Nouns and names

Use an apostrophe and s ('s) when something belongs to, is connected with or is done by someone or something:

- after a name:
  Barack Obama's presidency/party/policies

- after a singular noun:
  the **Government's** policies/popularity/mistakes

- after a name or singular noun ending with **s**:
  Keynes's economic theories/his **boss's** actions
  NOTE: Instead of using a word ending **s's**, you can create a different phrase:
  Mauritius's population → *The population of Mauritius*

- after a plural noun that does not end with 's':
  people's opinions

Use an apostrophe (but not s):

- after plural nouns that end with s:
  politicians' reactions/**girls'** and **boys'** ideas

Numbers

Do not use an apostrophe:

- with decades:
  the **1980s**

- with any other number (e.g. age):
  when he was in his **40s/forties**

- for plurals (e.g. products):
  Levi **501s**

Capital letters

Do not use an apostrophe:

- for plurals:
  CDs for sale

Use an apostrophe and s ('s):

- with the meaning 'belonging to', 'connected with' or 'done by', including when an organization ends with **s**
  The **CIA's** activities/the **IRS's** tax rules

Contracted verbs

Use an apostrophe when part of a verb is missing because it has been abbreviated:

the country's changing	→	the country is changing
it's changing	→	it is changing
they've decided	→	they have decided
you'll discover	→	you will discover
who's right?	→	who is right?
they couldn't respond	→	they could not respond

 Remember!

Contracted verbs are very commonly used in spoken language, but it is not a good idea to use them in academic work. Use the full forms. Doing so will also help you to avoid mistakes with apostrophes.

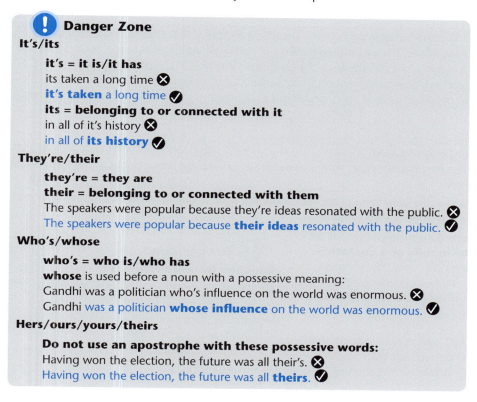

! Danger Zone

It's/its

> **it's = it is/it has**
> its taken a long time ✗
> **it's taken** a long time ✓
> **its = belonging to or connected with it**
> in all of it's history ✗
> in all of **its history** ✓

They're/their

> **they're = they are**
> **their = belonging to or connected with them**
> The speakers were popular because they're ideas resonated with the public. ✗
> The speakers were popular because **their ideas** resonated with the public. ✓

Who's/whose

> **who's = who is/who has**
> **whose** is used before a noun with a possessive meaning:
> Gandhi was a politician who's influence on the world was enormous. ✗
> Gandhi was a politician **whose influence** on the world was enormous. ✓

Hers/ours/yours/theirs

> **Do not use an apostrophe with these possessive words:**
> Having won the election, the future was all their's. ✗
> Having won the election, the future was all **theirs**. ✓

Exercises

1 Insert apostrophes in the correct places in the following sentences.

  a The beneficial effect of Vitamin D on childrens health has been noted in recent research findings.
  b Apparently, Ferraris latest supercar can reach speeds of over 200 miles per hour.
  c The development of teenagers identities is heavily influenced by their peers behaviour.
  d People have enjoyed Beethovens music for more than two hundred years.
  e Ive always believed that a designers approach should be to follow his or her intuition, rather than clients ideas.

2 Correct the following sentences by inserting or removing apostrophes where necessary. You may also need to change the form of some words.

  a Sales of DVD's rose rapidly during the period, and they're ascendancy over video's was soon confirmed.
  b Cinema-going reached its height in the 1940's, when its escapist appeal attracted audiences wanting to see movie stars who's lives seemed incredibly glamorous.
  c Boeing 747s are popular commercial aircraft, and many million's of travellers have used them.
  d Research into people in their 20's indicates that their's is the first generation to be confronted by this problem, and many of them cant find a way to deal with it.

24 Inverted commas

Inverted commas can be single (' ') or double (" "). When used for quoting actual words used by people in speech or written material, they are also called 'quotation marks' or 'speech marks'.

▶ Read this paragraph from a social studies essay and notice how inverted commas are used.

This report was considered 'ground-breaking' at the time because it indicated that changes in attitude at all levels of society were taking place. 'The established patterns of family life are being broken,' the report stated, 'and this is having a major impact on the lives of a great many people.' The report began by looking at what these 'established patterns' were and went on to detail the 'drastic changes' that were taking place. It concluded: 'Whether or not people in general are happy about it, the truth is that society is changing forever.'

Quoting

- Use a **colon** after a word meaning **said**:
  In their report, the researchers stated: 'Whether or not people in general are happy about it, the truth is that society is changing forever.'

  NOTE: Use a capital letter at the beginning of the quotation and a full stop at the end of it, both inside the inverted commas if the quotation is a full sentence.

- Use **two sets of inverted commas** if you put the speaker or writer **in the middle of a quotation**:
  'Our findings will have far-reaching consequences on the policy-makers,' the researchers stated in their report, 'as they suggest that current thinking is based on false assumptions.'

 **Danger Zone**
Omitting inverted commas

Always use inverted commas when you quote someone else's actual words. Failing to do so is regarded as plagiarism.

- Use **three dots** (brackets optional) to indicate that some of the quotation has been left out:
  'Our findings […] suggest that current thinking is based on false assumptions.'

- Put **inverted commas** at the beginning and end of a quoted phrase, to show that it is not your own words:
  The researchers pointed to the 'far-reaching consequences' of their findings.

- Use a **question mark** or **exclamation mark** *before* the second inverted comma if it is part of the quotation:
  'What would the consequences of their findings be for policy-makers?' the researchers asked.

  NOTE: There is no comma before the second inverted comma if a question mark or exclamation mark is used.

- Use a **full stop** after the second inverted comma if the quotation is not a whole sentence.
  The researchers said that current thinking was 'based on false assumptions'.

- Use a **comma** *and then* the second inverted comma if the sentence does not end with the quotation:
  'Our findings will have far-reaching consequences on policy-makers,' the researchers stated in their report.

Other uses of inverted commas

- For a **term** that **may not be generally known, used or understood**
  The researchers used an 'extremes filtering' method to collate the results of their survey. This involved removing people with the highest and lowest scores from their calculations.

- For the **title** of a book, report, magazine, film, painting, etc.
  The researchers published their report, 'Changing Demographics' in the journal 'Social Indicators'.

  NOTE: Both titles could be in italics, without inverted commas.

- To indicate that you believe that something **is not or may not be true**
  This kind of research is regarded as 'challenging the status quo' but it often has no impact on policy-makers.

- To **highlight a word or phrase to be focused on**, which has already been mentioned in the piece
  They make much of the potential impact of their report. But what exactly is this 'impact' likely to be?

 Remember!

If you are using single inverted commas throughout your work, use double inverted commas for any quotation within, or vice versa:

The researchers stated: 'We regard many current assumptions, especially those regarding what are commonly called "disadvantaged people", as both faulty and unhelpful.'

The researchers stated: "We regard many current assumptions, especially those regarding what are commonly called 'disadvantaged people', as both faulty and unhelpful."

There are no strict rules about whether you should use single or double, but be consistent.

Exercises

1 Decide whether or not these sentences are correctly punctuated, and correct those that are not.

a 'There are many different ways of accessing the information' the manual stated.
b In a letter to his family, he wrote: 'The thought has struck me that perhaps the artistic life is not for me'.
c He was once quoted as saying that he 'would never consider making a return to politics'.
d 'Why do certain people have these behaviour patterns?', she asks at the beginning of her paper.
e 'The case for equal rights,' she said in the speech, 'cannot be opposed in any real democracy.'
f One expert stated that the situation 'would not improve significantly … ' ' … for a considerable period of time.'

2 Add inverted commas where they are necessary or appropriate.

a In his paper The Impact of the Internet, he argued that too little attention was being paid to what he called the sudden intrusion. By this he meant the speed at which the internet took over people's lives. These days, he said, people have lost the ability to think for themselves and to use their own initiative.
b After the first day of conference, the leaders announced in their official statement: We feel that we have made significant progress towards a solution on this difficult question. They also spoke of the extremely cordial relations we enjoy. We anticipate a further announcement after tomorrow's meeting, they added.

25 Capital letters

 Writing Tip

Even if your writing is otherwise very good, failing to use capital letters where they are required, or using them where they should not be used, will spoil it.

When to use capital letters

People

the **name of a person**: Martin Simpson

a person's title, e.g. Mr, Mrs, Ms, Professor, President, Prime Minister, Sir, etc.: Professor Olivia Peters, President Nixon, Prime Minister

Places

a **building** or **landmark**: Westminster Abbey, Sydney Opera House

a **geographical feature**: the (River) Thames, Mount Everest, Yosemite National Park

a **street** or **district**: Hollywood Boulevard, the district of Kensington in London

the name of a **village/town/city**, **county**, **state** or **region**: Los Angeles, California, Scandinavia

a **country** or **continent**: the capital city of Wales, in Africa, the United Arab Emirates
NOTE: With **north**, **south**, **eastern**, **western**, **etc.** only use a capital if it is part of the name of a country or region: South Africa, South-East Asia, in the southern states of America

Days and months (but not seasons)

November/Saturday/in the winter

Planets

the Earth, Jupiter, Mars, the Moon

Nationalities and languages

French politicians, speak French/the Spanish

Historical periods and events

the Middle Ages, the Russian Revolution

Titles of published/media works

Books: *War and Peace, Lord of the Rings*

Films, TV programmes: *Titanic, Gone with the Wind, News at Ten, Who Wants to be a Millionaire?*

Magazines, newspapers, journals: *The Economist, Nature*

Articles and **academic papers:** in her article *'How Life has Changed for the Middle Classes'*

NOTE: In titles, small words such as 'a', 'the', 'and' or prepositions do not usually begin with capital letters, except when the first word of the title.

Job titles

the Head Teacher, the company's Chief Accountant, she has become Assistant Manager

NOTE: Do not use capital letters for a type of job, but only for the actual job title: She is a senior manager at the company.

Places of study and courses

the name of a **university, college, school**: the University of Sussex, Langland Comprehensive School.
NOTE: Do not a use a capital if you do not name the place: go to university, at school

departments: the English Faculty, the Drama Department

course titles: Applied Mathematics.
NOTE: Do not use capitals when talking generally about a subject area: A knowledge of statistics is vital for students.

examinations and qualifications: International Baccalaureate, A-Level, Bachelor of Arts

Organisations, official bodies and political parties, laws, treaties

Amnesty International, the Red Crescent, the Labour Party, Greenpeace, the European Union, the Geneva Convention, the Human Rights Act

Government institutions

Parliament, the House of Representatives, Congress, the Civil Service, the Department of Transport

NOTE: A capital letter is used to refer 'the Government' currently in power, but not to 'governments' in general.

Companies

Lloyd's Bank, Starbucks, Amazon

NOTE: 'Ltd' and 'plc' are usually used with full company names: Harston & Sons Ltd, Uniframe plc

Brand names

Google Play, Diet Coke, Ferrero Rocher

Abbreviations

Use capitals for **all** letters of abbreviations:

the BBC, the UN, UNESCO, NSPCC
the UK, the US Government
an MP, the CEO, the HR Department
CV, DVD, CD, PC
BSc, MBA

NOTE: The plural of any abbreviation has no apostrophe: MPs voted to …

An apostrophe is only used for a possessive: that CD's sales …

▸ See **23** *Apostrophes.*

 Remember!

- Use a capital letter to begin a sentence (and a full stop to end it).
  There are several reasons for this unusual turn of events.

- Use capital letters to address the person you are writing to in a letter or an email.
  Dear Mr Davies,

 Danger Zone

Misusing capital letters

- Do not use capital letters for ordinary nouns that cannot be regarded as names.
  This is a problem that affects Society in a great many ways. ✗
  This is a problem that affects society in a great many ways. ✓

- Do not use capital letters to emphasise a point, as you might in informal writing such as a text:
  This is an EXTREMELY IMPORTANT matter that has to be dealt with urgently. ✗
  This is an extremely important matter that has to be dealt with urgently. ✓

Exercise

1 Correct the following sentences by changing letters to capitals where necessary.

a Due to the screening of the mexican grand prix, this week's quiz show, 'send a line', will be broadcast on itv at the earlier time of 5.00 pm on friday.

b Farmers in the ivory coast live in poverty, while the cocoa they produce feeds the world's chocolate industry.

c The folk artist, steve knightly, mixes music and legend on his cd, 'cruel river'.

d Students wishing to go to university in north america are advised to take the international baccalaureate.

e The flood seriously affected homes in the north-west of England and completely destroyed the 100-year-old premises of grandacre and sons in preston.

f Last week, the uk border agency announced that it would be making a number of changes in line with the government's new policies.

g The renaissance was a period when great developments took place across europe in art and literature.

h In her paper, 'talking in twos', amanda pritchard examines a new approach to raising bilingual children.

26 Linking: contrasting

A **linker** is a word or phrase that connects sentences or parts of sentences.

But, however, **in spite of** and **on the other hand** are examples of **linkers**.

Writing Tip

Sophisticated and varied linking allows you to present contrasting ideas more clearly, and makes it easier for the reader to absorb information.

▶ **Read this introductory paragraph to an essay about the welfare state in Britain and look at how the ideas and points are connected.**

The welfare state in Britain was created immediately after the Second World War, but British society has changed a great deal since then. Aspects of the welfare state such as the NHS and the old-age pension, have been regarded as untouchable by every political party, but some experts say this should not continue to be the case. It is desirable to have a 'safety net' for the poorest in society, they say, but it is not economically sustainable for the taxpayer to fund all these benefits.

What's wrong: The linking of points and ideas is too basic and repetitive; everything is linked with 'but'.

- Here is the paragraph with better linking:

The welfare state in Britain was created immediately after the Second World War. **However**, British society has changed a great deal since then. **Although** aspects of the welfare state such as the NHS and the old-age pension, have been regarded as untouchable by every political party, some experts say this should not continue to be the case. **While** it is desirable to have a 'safety net' for the poorest in society, they say, it is not economically sustainable for the taxpayer to fund all these benefits.

- Here are some examples of how contrastive linkers can be used to improve the style of your writing.

Although/while/whereas

At the beginning of or between the clauses of a single sentence (with commas separating clauses):
Although/**While**/**Whereas** some historians regard it as a great success, others point to faults. OR

Some historians regard it as a great success, **although**/**while**/**whereas** others point to faults.

Remember!

Many words can be used instead of 'but' to link contrasting or contradictory points or pieces of information.

Even though

For greater emphasis than 'although':
Even though it is a key part of British society, the welfare state has its critics.

Whilst

More formal than 'while':
Whilst it is a key part of British society, the welfare state has its critics.

However

Here are the correct ways of using 'however'.

1 At the beginning of a new sentence, followed by a comma:
Some historians regard the welfare state as a great success. **However**, others point to faults. ✔
'However' cannot be used to join two parts of a single sentence.
Some historians regard it as a great success however others point to faults. ✘

NOTE: 'however' can also be used after a comma at the end of a sentence, particularly if it is short:
Others point to faults, **however**.

2 Within a second sentence, enclosed by commas:
Some historians regard the welfare state as a great success. Others, **however**, point to faults. ✔
'However' cannot be used as a linker without commas.
Some historians regard it as a great success. Others however point to faults. ✘

NOTE: 'However' can also be used with an adjective or adverb:
However successful the welfare state has been, it will always have its critics.

Nevertheless

At the beginning of a new sentence, followed by a comma; or in a second sentence, enclosed by commas:
The welfare state is a key part of British society. **Nevertheless**, it has its critics.
The welfare state is a key part of British society. People point out, **nevertheless**, that it does have many critics.

Despite/in spite of

Followed by 'the fact that', a noun, or '-ing' (with commas separating clauses):
Despite the fact that it is a key part of British society, the welfare state has its critics.
Despite its position as a key part of British society, the welfare state has its critics.
In spite of being a key part of British society, the welfare state has its critics.

Exercises

1 Rewrite these sentences using the linking words in brackets.

a The number of annual visitors to the Galapagos Islands is around 170,000, but in 1991 it was 41,000. (*begin with whilst*)

b Economic predictions are optimistic, but business confidence has fallen over the past few months. (*despite*)

c Weather data has been collected in Britain for 350 years, but opinions differ on how reliable that data is. (*however*)

d A dispersant was sprayed onto the oil slick, but thousands of seabirds were washed up along the beach. (*even though*)

e Some businesses invest heavily in researching new products, but others prefer to allocate more funds to marketing. (*whereas*)

2 Correct the following. Do not change the linking word or phrase used.

a It is a well-known fact that conservation projects can be costly nevertheless they need to be prioritised.

b Although some parents believe in the benefits of home tutoring. Most think that children require the school environment for the full development of their social skills.

c In spite of the medical profession give warnings people still smoke.

d Social-networking sites were designed to develop new friendships however their main use has been to communicate with existing peer groups.

e Whilst most film festivals in the world show one or two German movies but films 'Made in Germany' are not given the recognition they deserve.

27 Linking: adding

Not only were the existing facilities sub-standard, **but they were also** expensive to maintain.

▶ **Read this paragraph from a business case study and look at how the points are connected.**

Zolltrack modernised its factory in Thirsk and it invited management consultants Clarto to conduct an audit of its staff development provision and make recommendations. Very few Zolltrack staff had applied for funds to upgrade their qualifications, according to Clarto, and the internal workshops had little relevance to the actual needs of participants and were poorly attended.

What's wrong: The over-use of 'and' to link the ideas makes the linking too simplistic.

● Here is the paragraph with better linking:

In addition to modernising its factory in Thirsk, Zolltrack invited management consultants Clarto to conduct an audit of its staff-development provision and make recommendations. **Not only** had very few Zolltrack staff applied for funds to upgrade their qualifications, according to Clarto, **but also** the internal workshops had little relevance to the actual needs of participants, and were poorly attended.

● Here are some examples of how linkers for adding information are used.

Also/as well

Also is often used between a subject and a verb:
Although this essay will focus mainly on UK companies, it will **also** consider one or two French businesses.

As well is often used at the end of a sentence:
Although this essay will focus mainly on UK companies, it will consider one or two French businesses **as well**.

In addition to/as well as

At the beginning or in the middle of a sentence:

1 + '-ing'
In addition to/As well as buying up smaller companies, GVCY is expanding abroad.
GVCY is expanding abroad **in addition to/as well as buying** up smaller companies.

2 + noun
In addition to/As well as its factories in France, GVCY has a series of retail outlets in Switzerland.

Moreover/furthermore/in addition

At the beginning of a sentence followed by a comma, or later, enclosed by commas:
Zolltrack has improved its in-house staff development programme. **In addition**, more than 30 per cent of its workforce are now taking part-time courses at local colleges.
Zolltrack has improved its in-house staff development programme. More than 30 per cent of its workforce, **furthermore**, are now taking part-time courses at local colleges.

Not only ... but also

GVCY is **not only** a manufacturer **but also** a successful retailer of food products.
When **not only** is placed at the beginning for greater emphasis, you need to place the auxiliary or modal verb (*be, have could, will*, etc), if there is one, or a form of *do*, in front of the subject:

Not only **is GVCY** a manufacturer, but it is also a successful retailer of food products.
Not only **did GVCY expand** its operation in Europe, but it also formed a partnership in America.

 Danger Zone

Punctuation

It is a mistake to use linkers such as 'furthermore', 'moreover' or 'in addition' in the middle of a single sentence, without punctuation:

Zolltrack has improved its in-house staff development programme moreover more than 30 per cent of its workforce is now taking part-time courses at local colleges. ✖
Zolltrack has improved its in-house staff development programme; **moreover**, more than 30 per cent of its workforce is now taking part-time courses at local colleges. ✔

With

Used instead of an 'and' clause to give details about what is stated in the other part of the sentence:

1 + noun

The company had a very successful year, **with profits** of £3.2m. (= and it made/reported profits of ...)

2 + noun + '-ing'

The company had a very successful year, **with profits rising** from £1.7m to £3.3m. (= and profits rose from ...)

Exercises

1 Correct the following. Do not change the linking word or phrase used.

a Raw materials are becoming more expensive, in addition the costs of transporting them are increasing.
b As well as improving staff performance staff-development opportunities increase employees' loyalty.
c Not only Zolltrack is winning contracts in the private sector, it is also having success in the public sector.
d A new recruitment process was introduced, with its impressive results.
e Changing the factory's layout would be expensive. It could furthermore delay production.
f Having so far done most of its business in the UK, Zolltrack is now as well operating in America.

2 Rewrite the sentences, following the instructions in brackets.

a ACYG Solutions was declared bankrupt and its CEO was given a six-year prison sentence for fraud. (*Start with 'Not only ...'* .)
b GVCY made record profits in 2011 and it won an award for its staff-development programme. (*Start with 'As well as ...'.*)
c Zolltrack's braking system is the most technologically advanced on the market. At the moment, its system is also the cheapest. (*Add 'moreover' to the second sentence.*)
d Cornyt streamlined its management structure and 52 middle managers were made redundant. (*Use 'with' in the middle of the sentence.*)
e Grupmot plc has increased its market share in the UK and won new contracts in Spain. (*Use 'in addition to' in the middle of the sentence.*)

28   Linking: causes

result   linker   cause

There have been fewer accidents, **owing to** improved health and safety measures.

> **Writing Tip**
>
> In conversation, causes and results are often described using simple words like 'and', 'because' and 'so'. In academic writing, you will need to use a variety of more sophisticated words and phrases.

▶ Read this paragraph from a sociology essay and look at how the causes and results are connected.

The closure of a series of coal mines in the UK during the 1980s **brought about** a severe rise in regional unemployment. **Since** many of the pit towns had relied almost entirely on the local mine as a source of work, very few alternatives were available, **which explains why** many local men came to the conclusion that their working lives were finished.

Verbs

Cause/bring about/be responsible for

1 **+ noun phrase**
The Industrial Revolution **caused/brought about/was responsible for the growth** of the city.
The growth of cities in Britain **was caused/brought about by** the Industrial Revolution.

2 **+ object + infinitive**
The Industrial Revolution **caused people to leave** their villages for the city.

NOTE: 'Trigger' (to start a change) can also be used:
The Industrial Revolution **triggered** a series of changes …

Linkers connecting parts of a sentence

Because/because of

- because + subject + verb
  The slimming drug was withdrawn **because it had** serious long-term side effects.

- because of + noun phrase
  The slimming drug was withdrawn **because of its serious long-term side effects**.

As/since

often used at the beginning of a sentence to introduce a cause:
As/Since the slimming drug had serious long-term side effects, it was withdrawn.

Due to/owing to/on account of

1 **+ noun**
Due to/Owing to/On account of adverse publicity about its side effects, the slimming drug was withdrawn.

2 **+ noun + '-ing'**
Due to the slimming drug receiving adverse publicity about its side effects, it was withdrawn.

 **Danger Zone**

'Due to'/'owing to'/'On account of' are not followed by a subject, verb, etc.
Due to people were consuming so much junk food, instances of dangerous obesity increased.

You have to use one of the following grammatical structures:
On account of the high consumption of junk food, ... ✓
Owing to the fact that people were consuming so much junk food, ... ✓
Due to people consuming so much junk food, ... ✓

On the grounds that ...

= because; often used for the reason given by someone (the cause):

Experts called for an increase in the prices of alcoholic drinks in supermarkets **on the grounds that** this would reduce alcohol consumption.
On the grounds that it would reduce alcohol consumption, experts called for an increase in the prices of alcoholic drinks in supermarkets.

Which + be/explain + why

Many people work long hours, **which is**/**explains why** they often consume convenience foods.

Nouns

Cause (of) + noun phrase

The cause of hypothermia is normally an overexposure to extremely cold temperatures.

Reason for + noun phrase/reason why + subject, verb, etc.

The main **reason for the improvement** in the patients' cardiovascular function was the course of aerobic exercise that they had undertaken.
The main **reason why the patients' cardiovascular function improved** was the course of aerobic exercise that they had undertaken.

Exercises

1 Identify and correct the mistakes in these sentences.

   a Crime rates have risen in this part of the city, and is why so many residents have sold up and left.
   b On account of the museum able to attract private sponsorship, its short-term future seems secure.
   c The media's new power to question and criticise may have brought a lack of respect for politicians.
   d The research facility was closed because serious concerns about its standards of health and safety.
   e One reason of an episode of hyperactivity in children may be the excessive consumption of sugar.
   f A number of basic errors were made due to no trained medical staff were present at the time.

2 Rewrite the sentences, using the words in brackets.

   a Many citizens are dissatisfied with the way in which lobbyists influence government policy. This means that there are often calls for reform. (*Since*)
   b Some adolescents appear to suffer from headaches and anxiety because of their repeated poor performance in computer games. (*due*)
   c Because it would affect their trade, local shopkeepers attacked the new parking charge. (*grounds*)
   d Syms argues that an apparently trivial event may cause a period of mental illness. (*triggered*)

29 Linking: results

cause	linking verb	result
There were too many layers of management,	which **led to**	a decrease in efficiency

> ### Writing Tip
> Try to vary the way you link results and their causes and to clarify their relative importance. Sometimes it is necessary to emphasise the result, rather than the cause, as in the example above.

▶ Read this paragraph on stress in the workplace and look at how results and their causes are connected.

> Burnout in the workplace can happen **as a result of** prolonged stress. Initial symptoms may **stem from** the desire of an employee to do well and to fit into the corporate structure. An unrealistic deadline from a senior manager can then **lead to** additional pressure on the individual, which may become **so severe that** he or she is unable to continue functioning in the workplace.

Verbs

Result from/stem from

followed by the cause of something:

1 + noun

An inability to think clearly at work may simply **result**/**stem from** a lack of sleep.

2 + object + '-ing'

Stress at work can **result from employees feeling** that they are badly treated by management.

Lead to/result in

followed by the result:

1 + noun

Changes in management and systems **led to**/**resulted in** problems for many of the staff.

2 + object + '-ing'

Changes in management and systems **led to**/**resulted in** some employees leaving the company.

3 the present participle (-ing form)

There were constant personnel changes, **leading to**/**resulting in** confusion among staff.

Linkers connecting clauses and sentences

So/such ... that ...

used for linking a cause with its result in these patterns:

1 so + adjective/adverb + that

Change was **so rapid that** many employees struggled to keep pace with it.

Change was introduced **so rapidly that** many employees struggled to keep pace with it.

2 such + noun + that

There was **such rapid change that** many employees struggled to keep pace with it.

> ### Danger Zone
>
> **Confusing 'so' and 'such'**
>
> **So** is used with an adjective or adverb; **such** is used with a noun or noun phrase.
>
> Systems changed in so short time that employees became confused. ✖
>
> Systems changed **so rapidly/in such a short time** that employees became confused.

As a result

- At the beginning of a second sentence, followed by a comma:

  The company culture became more authoritarian and less caring. **As a result**, morale among staff fell.

- Mid-sentence, after 'and', with commas before and after:

  The company culture became more authoritarian and, **as a result**, morale among staff fell.

- Also in these patterns, in a single sentence:

  1 as a result of (+ noun) + '-ing'

  As a result of the company changing its culture, morale among staff fell.

  2 as a result of which/with the result that

  The company culture became more authoritarian and less caring, **as a result of which**/**with the result that** morale among staff fell.

Therefore/consequently

At the beginning of a second sentence, followed by a comma or later in a second sentence, with commas if they come after the verb:

Key members of staff felt too pressured by their bosses. **Therefore/Consequently**, many of them left and joined rival firms. OR Many of them **therefore/consequently** left and joined firms. OR Many of them left, **therefore/consequently**, and joined rival firms.

Thus

= therefore, more formal but appropriate for academic writing:

Staff numbers were significantly reduced. **Thus**, those that remained were put under enormous pressure.

Thus/thereby + '-ing'

linking a result with its cause:

Management did not reduce the overall workload, **thus/thereby putting** remaining members of staff under enormous pressure.

Which/this + mean that

Staff numbers were reduced, **which meant that** remaining employees had bigger workloads.
Staff numbers were reduced. **This meant that** remaining employees had bigger workloads.

Nouns

Consequence (of)/result (of)/outcome (of) + noun phrase

An inevitable **consequence/result/outcome of** the increase in online fraud is the growing number of companies offering software solutions to the problem.

Exercises

1 Identify and correct the mistakes in these sentences.

a Unemployment in the region was high that the Government felt obliged to establish an enterprise zone.
b The digital revolution has led a much wider range of programme choices for the consumer.
c Accidents in laboratories may result in a lack of supervision.
d Funding for the arts fell therefore many groups and organisations were unable to continue.
e Employment opportunities in the sector fell, resulted in increased competition for jobs.
f Dickens regularly gave talks and readings, thereby raised his public profile.

2 Rewrite these sentences, using the words in brackets.

a As both of the town's electronics factories were forced to close during the recession, the only employment opportunities to be found are in the service and public sectors. (*as a result*)
b Riots continued for ten days. As a result, many villages were left in ruins. (*which meant that*)
c Radiation leaks at the Chernobyl plant were caused by the absence of a confinement shell. (*resulted*)
d The cause of Seasonal Affective Disorder (SAD) seems to be a shortage of sunlight. (*stem*)

30 Signposting

Certain words and phrases act as **signposts** to point your reader to other parts of your essay.

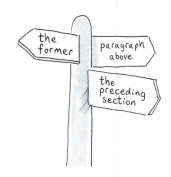

> **Writing Tip**
>
> A coherent piece of writing, such as an essay, works as a whole rather than as a series of separate points, and should have a clear line of development, marked by 'signposting' language.

▶ Look at this paragraph with three signposting words or phrases.

> Japan and the United Kingdom, with an emperor and a monarch as head of state **respectively**, are sometimes compared with each other. **The former country** remained culturally isolated for a long period of its history, while **the latter** evolved through its engagements, peaceful and military, with the world. Despite these differences, there are some interesting similarities.

All three of these words or phrases refer backwards to earlier parts of the text. Not only do they help you to avoid repetition, but they also serve, in the reader's mind, to link one part of your writing to another.

Respectively

This word is used to mean 'the order in which I mentioned them'. In the paragraph above, it tells the reader that Japan has an emperor as head of state, and the United Kingdom has a monarch.

It can be used at the end of a clause (as in the text above) or earlier in the sentence:

'Sevilo' (from Savile Row) and 'nekutai' are, **respectively**, the Japanese words for a Western style business suit and a tie (or necktie).

The former, the latter

If you have mentioned two things in your writing and want to refer back to them:

the former → 'the first one mentioned'
the latter → 'the second and last one mentioned'

In the paragraph above: the former country = Japan; the latter = the United Kingdom.

- 'The former' and 'the latter' can precede a noun: **the former country** remained culturally isolated …; or, if the meaning is clear, stand alone: while **the latter** evolved through its engagements …

- You can use these phrases as a pair as in the text above, or you can use them on their own:

  In the middle of the 19th century, Japan opened itself to trade and ended its feudal system. **The former** development initially brought chaos, as foreign traders exploited the currency's unrealistic exchange rate between gold and silver.

  'the former development' = Japan opening itself to trade

Other words and phrases that refer backwards

You can use **above** to refer to something immediately before or something anywhere before:

The rapid growth in the Sony Corporation during the 1960s can be seen in the graph **above**.
In the part of this essay **above** on political change, it may have been implied that the transition to a capitalist economy occurred without opposition.

The following words and expressions can also be used for referring backwards:

- reference to the part immediately before:
  In the preceding/**previous** section of this report a comparison was made between …

- reference to a specific part before:
  As we saw in the first three paragraphs/in the opening section of this essay …

- reference to a specific point before:
  The two parties could not agree on the terms of the treaty, and **this disagreement** lasted three years …
  ▶ See 31 *Using pronouns correctly*

Words and phrases that refer forwards

You can use **below** to refer to information that comes immediately afterwards or later on in the text:

Several of the accounts described **below**, of early visits to Japan by English travellers, focus on ceremonial aspects of the culture.

The following expressions can also be used for referring forwards:

- reference to the part immediately afterwards:
  In the following paragraph, the expansion of trade between Japan and its neighbours will be discussed.

- reference to a specific part to come:
  As we shall see in the second half of this essay, …

- general reference forwards:
  As we shall see, there are some distinct differences between …

 **Remember!**

A specialised form of signposting language occurs in the section of an essay where you state its 'scope':
The first part of this essay will examine the causes of …; then it will consider …; etc.

▶ See 'Stating the scope' in **48** *The language of argument.*

Exercises

1 Choose the correct alternative to complete the sentences.

a As we saw in the ………… (*following/preceding*) section of this report, Portugal has suffered a decline in its export productivity.

b Revenues from agriculture and tourism were mainstays in the Spanish economy. Indeed, income from the ………… (*latter/former*) source continued to increase as holidaymakers took advantage of package offers. The boom period eventually came to an end, however, as we shall see in the ………… (*following/preceding*) paragraph.

c As we saw …………, (*below/above*) three factors combined to produce Ireland's financial crisis.

d Visitors to Greece are attracted by its historical sites and its beaches. The ………… (*latter/former*) include ancient temples and Byzantine monasteries.

2 Rewrite the sentences using the words in brackets.

a In the preceding paragraph, we saw how Milan emerged as Italy's most important commercial centre. (*above*)

b After Paris, Lyon is the second biggest city in France and Marseille is the third biggest city. (*respectively*)

c By exploring the statistics in the table that follows, it will be possible to appreciate the scale of Germany's postwar recovery. (*below*)

d There is a certain amount of rivalry between Madrid and Barcelona. Madrid is the centre of power, while Barcelona often regards itself as the economic driving force of the country. (*the former …/the latter …*)

A pronoun (e.g. **its, they, this, that, she, them**) is a word that is used instead of a noun or name to refer to people and things.

> A short presentation can be more effective than a long talk because the audience may lose track of <u>its</u> main point.

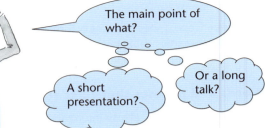

The main point of what?

A short presentation?

Or a long talk?

 Writing Tip

Always re-read your sentences to make sure that any pronoun references are clear. Small mistakes can cause significant confusion for your reader, as this example shows.

Using a pronoun carefully to avoid confusion

▶ **Look at this sentence from an essay on EU business activity.**

Both parties signed the contract at the same time as the agreement and passed it to the lawyers. ✖

What's wrong: It must be clear what 'it' refers to: *the contract* or *the agreement*. Here are two possible ways of doing this:

Both parties signed the contract at the same time as the agreement and passed **the contract** to the lawyers. ✔
Both parties signed the contract at the same time as the agreement and passed **the former** to the lawyers. ✔

 ◗ See 'The former, the latter' in **30** *Signposting*.

Using personal pronouns (e.g. his, her, him; their, theirs, them)

▶ **Look at this sentence and find the mistake.**

The CEO asked his accounts manager why he had not been notified of the changes in EU regulations. ✖

What's wrong: It is not clear who 'he' refers to: *the CEO* or *the accounts manager*. Here is a way of correcting this:

The CEO asked his accounts manager why he had not notified him of the changes in EU regulations. ✔

▶ **Look at this sentence and find a better way of expressing it.**

A senior manager is responsible for the actions of his team. ✖

What's wrong: The writer has used *his*, but the senior manager could be a woman. Use one of these alternatives:

Senior managers are responsible for the actions of their teams. ✔
A senior manager is responsible for the actions of their team. ✔

 Remember!

Don't use 'them' instead of 'those'.
Many companies have stopped producing ~~them~~ **those** goods.

Using this, these; that, those

- In academic writing, *this* and *these* are often used on their own to refer back to a noun phrase:

> The possibilities for conflict are always present in the relationship between line managers and their staff, but **these** (= 'the possibilities for conflict') can be managed in a number of different ways.

- *this* is also frequently used on its own to refer to a complete idea:

> Consumer loyalty can be crucial to the success of a brand. **This** is clear from a recent study in *The Economist*.

- *this* and *these* may be used with an appropriate 'summarising noun':

> The Government plans to support small businesses by cutting some of the bureaucracy that makes it difficult for them to respond quickly to new situations. **This policy** has been supported by the CBI.

> The company's CEO suggested that the factory in Dundee could be sold off, and that the workforce in Newcastle could be cut by a third. The trustees, however, did not support **these proposals**.

Common summarising nouns include the following:

advice argument claim crisis criticism description development disagreement discussion estimate example explanation idea increase issue measure objective phenomenon policy problem proposal reduction remark situation subject suggestion system trend view warning

- **that/those + of** and **those + who/which/that** are used when the thing in question is defined afterwards:
  The process of setting objectives is similar to **that** (= **the process**) of determining a brand identity.
  Retail experts describe two types of consumer: **those** (= **consumers**) who know exactly what they are looking for, and **those** (= **consumers**) who hope to be inspired by what they see.

Using such

such a + singular noun and **such + plural/uncountable noun** mean 'of the kind/type already mentioned':
An impressive headquarters can be a major asset to a business – if **such a building** can be acquired.
Green business methods can be expensive, but **such methods** can enhance a company's image.

Exercises

1 Improve the sentences by replacing the underlined pronouns.

a Senior managers took their staff to a hotel, where <u>they</u> gave presentations. (NOTE: The senior managers gave the presentations.)

b To do <u>their</u> job well, a human resources manager needs imagination as well as knowledge of procedures.

c The conference on performance management ended with a keynote speech. <u>It</u> was a great success, according to those who attended. (NOTE: The keynote speech was a great success.)

d A council of student representatives was formed, and <u>their</u> task was to liaise with the student body.

2 Choose the more appropriate options.

a Several senior managers pointed out the risks if the business expanded too fast. These *explanations/warnings* were ignored, however, by the CEO.

b More and more SMEs are seeking business abroad. This *trend/proposal* is a reflection of the lack of opportunities in the UK.

c Regulations to prevent the import of certain foodstuffs have been put in place at UK borders. These *objectives/measures* are designed to protect public health.

d A recent study suggests that employees with the same political views as their senior managers are more likely to be promoted. This *system/phenomenon* was, however, first described twenty years ago.

32 Avoiding repetition of words

It may take homeless people some time to acquire a permanent address, but they can apply for a job more easily once they **have done so**.

 Writing Tip

It is important to avoid repetition in your writing and to make your writing as clear and coherent as possible. Use the techniques outlined in this unit, along with those in units **30** and **31** to help you achieve this. Read through your writing. If you find that you have overused a word or phrase, find an alternative, such as a synonym or pronoun.

Using substitute words

- You can use **one/one(s)** to avoid repeating nouns:

Unlike other housing projects in the area, the <u>housing project</u> in Philadelphia evolved through the equal participation of the Mayor's office and the local community.

Unlike other housing projects in the area, **the one** in Philadelphia …

- In formal writing, it is common to avoid repeating a verb phrase by using the appropriate form of **do + so**:

The charity converted several disused car parks into winter soup kitchens. When it had <u>converted the car parks</u>, it was able to provide daily meals for more than 200 people.

The charity converted several disused car parks into winter soup kitchens. When it **had done so**, it was able to provide daily meals for more than 200 people.

Omitting unnecessary words

- You can leave out the noun after words such as **both, few, many** and **some,** which describe 'how many':

Many council workers feel sympathy for homeless members of their community, but few <u>council workers</u> respond to the problem, as Mike Forster did, by setting up a shelter.

Many council workers feel sympathy for homeless members of their community, but **few** respond to the problem, as Mike Forster did, by setting up a shelter.

- If the meaning is clear, you can leave out the noun **when it follows an adjective**:

There are two short-term solutions to the problem of homelessness. The first <u>solution</u> involves converting empty properties into viable accommodation.

There are two short-term solutions to the problem of homelessness. The **first** involves converting empty properties into viable accommodation.

A Government spokesperson praised the schemes that the charity had set up, and some of the most successful <u>schemes</u> were later adopted nationally.

A Government spokesperson praised the schemes that the charity had set up, and **some of the most successful** (ones) were later adopted nationally.

Using synonyms

Synonyms not only help you avoid repetition, they also show that you can vary the words you use.

▶ Read this paragraph and find the synonyms that the writer uses to avoid repeating the words or phrases in bold.

> Stephen Day, one of the authors of the report on **the hostel,** began working in Liberia as a freelance journalist, but soon became involved in various aid projects. This led to the **setting up** of his own hostel for homeless **boys.** Once established, the house became a refuge for young men, many of whom had run away from abusive fathers. Its success seems to have derived from a **combination** of basic discipline and an attempt to bring the boys into the decision-making processes used in running the hostel. Together, these two aspects of the daily life in their new accommodation helped the troubled youths to regain some elements of self-respect.

- Here are the synonyms:
  the hostel → *the house* → *their new accommodation*
  setting up → *established*
  boys → *young men* → *the troubled youths*
  combination → *these two aspects*

Exercises

1 Amend the sentences to avoid repetition.

a Most young people make compromises with their parents that allow the family to work as an entity, but some teenagers seem unable to make compromises.

b The two housing trusts decided to merge in 2020. Both housing trusts believed that working together would improve outcomes.

c Of all the charities working with homeless people, the charity whose name is most familiar to the public is Shelter.

d There have been many attempts to renovate empty housing stock and make it available to families in need. The latest attempt has been sponsored by the property group Campton Holdings.

e Stableton Ltd agreed in 2016 to improve the living conditions of its 540 tenants in Islington, but when an inspection took place in 2018, it was evident that the firm had not improved the living conditions.

2 Rewrite this paragraph using synonyms to replace the underlined words.

The charity Homes for People invested some of its savings in a business with a scheme for constructing ecological housing on a site outside Leeds. The <u>site</u> for the <u>scheme</u> seemed ideal, but it became apparent after six months that very <u>little housing</u> was actually being <u>constructed</u>. When the charity contacted the <u>business</u> to establish why <u>six months</u> had elapsed without any obvious progress, it discovered that the entire <u>scheme</u> had been sub-contracted to a smaller <u>business</u>.

33   Parallel structures

Some sentences involve repeating the same grammatical structure to link points. Repeated grammatical forms of this kind are called **parallel structures**.

The student was accepted on to the course because **he had** <u>the correct language level</u> **and** (he had) <u>the required school exam results</u>.	→ The underlined noun phrases link back to 'he had'. It is not necessary to repeat 'he had'.

 Writing Tip

Parallel structures enable you to integrate lists of ideas into long, coherent, well-formed sentences.

Parallel forms

- Here is an example of a parallel structure using infinitive verb forms.

Television was originally **designed to** <u>educate</u>, (to) <u>inform</u> **and** (to) <u>entertain</u> the masses.	→ The underlined verbs all link back to 'designed to', though it is not necessary to repeat 'to'.

▶ **Read the sentence below on the subject of new media. What error has the student made?**

There is evidence that excessive use of new media among children can affect their performance at school, influence their behaviour at home and limiting their overall attention span. ✖

What's wrong: The first two verbs 'affect' and 'influence' are parallel. They are not in the singular form because they go together with 'can'. The third verb should therefore be in the same form as 'affect' as it is also linked with 'can' → 'can limit'.

- Here is the sentence with parallel structures:

There is evidence that excessive use of new media among children **can affect** their performance at school, **influence** their behaviour at home **and limit** their attention span. ✔

- Here are some more complex examples of sentences with parallel structures:

Despite <u>spending</u> many hours a day on computer games consoles and <u>hardly ever reading</u>, some of the teenagers had high reading comprehension scores.

NOTE: 'despite' is followed by the '-ing' form of a verb. 'Reading' is in the same form because this part of the sentence means 'despite hardly ever reading'.

Some experts **recommend that** <u>parents should restrict home computer use</u> **and that** this use <u>should always be supervised</u> by parents.

NOTE: 'that' is repeated because the first underlined section is about 'parents', whereas the second underlined section is about the 'use' of computers. In other words, the subject in each clause is different.

Home computer use **proved** <u>to be a significant factor</u> in performance in tests and <u>to have an influence</u> on behaviour in the classroom.

NOTE: 'to' must be repeated because 'to be' and 'to have' form part of two separate phrases: 'to be a factor in'/'to have an influence on'.

Neither/nor

This structure is used for expressing two connected negatives, but the verbs used are not negative and both of them must be in the same form:

Findings from research into the effects of internet use **are neither consistent nor indicative of** any major problem. ✔

▶ See **12** *Negative words and phrases.*

Note also the word order when using 'neither'/'nor' in this way.

Exercises

1 Underline the parallel forms in the sentences.

a Many companies are using call centres in India to promote products, deal with enquiries and complaints, and monitor consumer behaviour.

b Unlike humans, animals have an acute sense of smell and, if they need food, know where to find it.

c As young people spend more and more time on media-based websites, celebrity culture is being blamed for an increase in materialism and a fall in creativity.

d In some countries, streets have been transformed from car-centred areas to social spaces in which neighbours meet, children play, and the car driver is an occasional visitor.

e Unfortunately, neither using the internet to shop, nor going through a self-service checkout, speeds up supermarket shopping.

2 Correct or improve the students' sentences by using parallel structures.

a The course syllabus includes an analysis of the concept of innovation, designing technical images and you will prepare project specifications.

b The music is entitled 'Before Dawn', which was written by Dominique Ferris and published in 2010.

c The research will investigate the number of people leaving school early and get married.

d Equipment has to be bought, laboratories set up and hiring of staff is done before any work can begin.

e Global air travel is safe, convenience and more efficiency of fuel than it used to be.

3 Turn each set of notes into a single sentence with parallel structures.

(a)

> *Benefits of team work:*
>
> – *mix with different personality types*
>
> – *pooling ideas*
>
> – *joint decisions*

(b)

> *Successful marketing strategy:*
>
> – *objectives: clear*
>
> – *advertising campaign (wide-ranging)*
>
> – *public support: strong*

34 Participles

What are participles?

A present participle is a form of a verb ending with '-ing' → *facing*

A past participle is often a form of a verb ending with '-ed' → *worked*

Many common past participles do not end in '-ed' (e.g. *done, driven, known*)

A past participle can also be used after 'having' → *having worked, having done*

> **Writing Tip**
>
> Using participles enables you to produce sophisticated sentences that connect important pieces of information. This can be more effective than writing short simple sentences or linking these using simple conjunctions such as 'and', 'then' or 'because'.

▶ **Look at the ways you can use participles.**

1 To describe causes and results

The country's car industry was obliged to restructure in the 1990s because it faced the effects of a recession.

→ **Facing** the effects of a recession in the early 1990s, the country's car industry was obliged to restructure.

2 To give important additional information

Exports grew over the next few years. They were driven by an international marketing campaign.

→ Exports, **driven** by an international marketing campaign, grew over the next few years.

3 To present a sequence of events

Michael Tadakis worked in the travel industry. Then he formed his own company in 2017.

→ Michael Tadakis formed his own company in 2017, **having** previously **worked** in the travel industry.

▶ **Read this sentence about shareholders.**

Having gained a 28 per cent market share in the UK, shareholders were very pleased with the company's performance. ✖

What's wrong: The sentence does not make sense. The subject of the participle ('Having gained') is not the same as the subject of the rest of the sentence and the verb 'were'. The shareholders did not gain the market share: the company did.

> **Remember!**
>
> The subject of the participle must be the same as the main subject of the sentence as a whole. To illustrate this, the subjects have been underlined in the three examples above.

● The subject should be consistent and be either the shareholders or the company:

The UK shareholders were very pleased with the company's performance, having been told that it had gained a 28 per cent market share. ✔

Having gained a 28 per cent market share in the UK, the company made a special announcement to delighted shareholders. ✔

 **Danger Zone**

Participle/subject confusion

A sentence using a participle must be carefully constructed so that it makes sense. Look at these two pieces of information:

The company adjusted to changing market conditions. It produced new products and introduced new systems.

Adjusting to changing market conditions, **the company produced** new products and **introduced** new systems. (= *The company adjusted, produced and introduced*). ✔

Adjusting to changing market conditions, new products were produced and new systems were introduced.
(*The products and systems did not adjust. The parts of the sentence do not correctly relate to each other.*)

Exercises

1 Decide if these sentences are correct or not.

a Spotting a gap in the market, a new model was launched in 2020.
b The CEO, having called in a firm of consultants, decided to restructure the company.
c Written in 2017, he had a huge success with his autobiography.
d The budget, designed to accommodate some seasonal variation in prices, was still an underestimate.
e Having sought the opinions of leading investors, the proposed merger was abandoned.
f The private sector created a range of new jobs, satisfying the needs of government policy.

2 Write single sentences using participles.

a They carried out extensive market research. Then they launched the new product.
b The management wished to streamline the operation. Therefore they reduced staffing.
c Competitors overtook the company in terms of market share. It had to respond quickly.
d The garage began to struggle. It was experiencing keen competition from other companies.
e The officers drew up a shortlist of candidates. Then they passed it to the manager for review.
f Customer satisfaction rose to an all-time high during the holiday period. It was monitored by in-store complaints records.

3 Turn the notes about companies into sentences with participles. Use two sentences for each note.

1

Jagsta plc:
– lost market share
– made 100 staff redundant
– operated as a smaller company
– returned to profitability

2

Bulltop Construction Ltd:
– founded in 2008
– grew quickly
– landed a major public-sector contract in 2009
– moved to new premises

Although participants were chosen for the experiment from a wide variety of backgrounds.

What does this mean? Has anyone seen the main clause of this sentence?

💡 Writing Tip

Make sure that every sentence you write really is a complete sentence. An incomplete sentence is a serious error that may give the reader a very bad impression of your work.

▶ **Read this extract from a science essay and think about which sentences are complete and which are incomplete.**

The results of the experiment were consistent. Regardless of the background of the subjects. Or the time-frame over which the experiment was conducted. The researchers were therefore able to draw firm conclusions from the experiment. These were not universally accepted in the scientific world. Because they contradicted previous research.

What's wrong: The second, third and last 'sentences' are not complete. They are all clauses that cannot stand alone.

● Here is the extract with complete sentences throughout:

The results of the experiment were consistent, regardless of the background of the subjects or the time-frame over which the experiment was conducted. The researchers were therefore able to draw firm conclusions from the experiment. These were not universally accepted in the scientific world, because they contradicted previous research.

● To be complete, a sentence needs to have **a subject** and **a main verb**. As such, it carries an idea and makes sense on its own.
  ▶ See **2** *Parts of a sentence.*

In the first sentence of the correct paragraph above, 'results' is the subject and 'were' is the main verb.

Extra information

The results of the experiment   were consistent …   +   regardless of the background of the subjects.

subject   main verb   +   regardless of the time frame over which the
                                                            experiment was conducted.

The extra pieces of information have no main verb. They are not complete sentences that make sense on their own.

● A complete sentence can begin with a **linking word**, but the sentence then has to have **another clause**: Because they contradicted a lot of previous research in the area. ✗

◆ Decide what's wrong with the sentences on the left, before looking at the explanations on the right.

Not a very good example of most research in the field. ✖	→	*There is no subject or main verb; this is a phrase, not a sentence.*
Rather than the kind of research which would have widespread applications. ✖	→	*This presents an alternative but does not say to what and so makes no sense on its own.*
Hard to be sure whether the research results are reliable. ✖	→	*This has no main subject or verb; it is more like an informal spoken statement. To be complete, it should start 'It is …'*

 Danger Zone

Writing in the way you think

You do not always think in complete sentences! Here's what you might think if you were writing an essay:
The experiment was conducted on adults and children. Didn't make any difference. Same results for both groups. ✖

These thoughts are incomplete sentences. Here is one way of presenting them in the essay:
The experiment was conducted on adults and children, but this made no difference to the results, which were the same for both groups. ✔

Exercises

1 Decide whether these sentences are complete or incomplete.

a In spite of all the changes that had taken place and how much the situation had altered in the intervening years.

b With the arrival of environmental engineering, approaches to some projects required fresh thinking.

c Projects achieved by teams without argument are rare.

d Using statistics to confuse the reader as much as anything else.

e Supposedly the most successful research and development laboratory in the UK.

f Hoping for a result before the morning, some of the team went without sleep.

2 Read these paragraphs and underline the incomplete sentences. Then rewrite the paragraphs so that they contain only complete sentences.

To do this you may need to add linking devices to join some sentences, create conditional, relative or participle clauses, and/or reword some parts.

a The jury system is a central plank of the British legal system. A number of critics of it who say that it is outdated. Many cases too complex for ordinary members of the public. The result – they feel that juries should not be used any longer.

b A number of reasons why the ruling party might lose the next election. The state of the economy is probably the top one. Many people are losing their jobs and businesses are unable to attract investment. A growing loss of faith in the Government.

c A backbench MP can rise to prominence. He or she makes an exceptional speech. It's reported in the press. Or by chairing a committee. Particularly when the committee interviews public figures.

d TV watchers could not believe how many people the protest attracted. Despite one of the wettest days of the year. On every street in the city centre, hundreds of protestors. Carrying slogans and denounced the Government's policies.

▶ **Read this sentence from an essay on management systems.**

In a management system such as this, staff become chiefly concerned with pleasing their managers and they get stressed and they lose focus on the needs of the company and they are unable to carry out core operations in the best possible way, so the system is acting to the detriment of the organisation.

What's wrong: The sentence is garbled, with too much repetition of 'and'.

There are several ways that you can avoid writing long sentences that are disorganised and confusing for your reader.

Using appropriate linkers

● You can create two or more sentences, with clear linking, instead of one very long sentence:

In a management system such as this, staff become chiefly concerned with pleasing their managers. **This causes** them to get stressed and to lose focus on the needs of the company. **As a result**, they are unable to carry out core operations in the best possible way and therefore the system is acting to the detriment of the organisation.

Using parallel structures and appropriate punctuation

● You can present a coherent list using parallel structures, a colon and semicolons, and separate this from any further points or information:

A management system such as this has a number of negative effects on staff: **they become** chiefly concerned with pleasing their managers; **they get stressed**; **they lose focus** on the needs of the company; and **they are unable** to carry out core operations in the best possible way. **This means** that the system is acting to the detriment of the organisation.

◗ See **33** *Parallel structures* and **21** *Colons and semicolons*.

▶ **Read this sentence from an essay on management theories.**

Sceptics regard management theories as fads that do more harm than good because companies copy each other without thinking and they change systems so that they conform to the latest management theory but there is no clear evidence that the theory really works and even if it is a good one, it might not work for every organisation.

The sentence contains the following points:
1 the general view of sceptics
2 what sceptics think companies do
3 why sceptics think companies shouldn't do that.

This is too much for a single sentence. The three points need to be made in a coherent, **easy-to-read** way. To do this, they need to be clearly separated into their own sentences:

> Sceptics regard management theories as fads that do more harm than good. **They believe** that companies copy each other without thinking **and change** systems so that they conform to the latest management theory. **However,** according to the sceptics, there may be no clear evidence that the theory really works, and even if it is a good one, it might not work for every organisation.

 Remember!

Always read your sentences through after you have written them to make sure that the points are clearly presented. Ask yourself:

- *Would it be hard to read the sentence aloud in a way that makes clear sense?*
- *Does it have to be read again in order to be understood?*

Exercises

1 Rewrite the following disorganised sentences as two separate sentences.

a Studies of youth culture in Britain always tend to focus on the 1960s as that is the period when many changes were clearly visible in British society and when the whole subject became a matter of public debate and in fact many of these developments actually began in the 1950s and any study of youth culture should really begin in that decade.

b The difference between sociological and journalistic approaches to events is that in the first approach sociologists have to use scientific methods to gather their information unlike journalists who can easily write up information without witnessing the actual event which makes them biased sometimes.

c Prime Ministers are like senior managers in that they can delegate much of their power to individual departments and focus their energy instead on overall strategy and presentation or they can micro-manage the individual decisions of their department heads but if they choose this route, they risk being overwhelmed by the sheer scale of modern government.

2 Decide whether these sentences are clear or disorganised, and rewrite the disorganised ones as two sentences.

a George Orwell is chiefly known for his novels *Animal Farm* and *Nineteen Eighty-Four* and these are still widely read today and he also wrote a great deal of journalism and his journalism is very important, for example *The Road to Wigan Pier* about the life of miners and the relevance of socialism.

b The Equality in Employment Act prevents employers from discriminating against people on the grounds of their age, either by not offering them a job which they are qualified to do or by enforcing early retirement against their wishes.

c It has been argued, with the benefit of graphic anecdotes, that organisations are hampered by health and safety legislation and when individual elements of the law are closely examined, it becomes clear, and there is an exaggerated interpretation by managers causing the problem rather than the code itself.

A short sentence can draw attention to important information.   →   **Films can change people's lives.** They have the power to inspire, educate and inform people about the world and they can do this in a number of different ways.

Too many short sentences, however, can reduce the impact of a key idea.   →   Films can affect people in a number of different ways. They can inspire people to achieve great things. They can also educate people about events. Films are a useful way of providing information about the world. Films can change people's lives.

 Writing Tip

Too many short sentences can create a bad impression, especially if there are several together. Before you start writing, it may be a good idea to make brief notes of what you are going to include and then to think of ways of joining your ideas together to produce sentences that have an appropriately academic style.

▶ **Read this extract from an essay on cinema.**

> Orson Welles was a prodigy in the world of film. He directed *Citizen Kane* at the age of 26. He starred in it too. Many people think it is the greatest film ever made. That was in 1941. He made a number of other films then. Some of them are considered masterpieces as well.

What's wrong: The information reads like notes and does not flow. Some of the sentences need to be joined together, using appropriate ways of linking.

● Here is the extract with the sentences linked together:

> Orson Welles was a prodigy in the world of film. In 1941, at the age of 26, he directed and starred in *Citizen Kane*, considered by many people to be the greatest film ever made. He subsequently made a number of other films, some of which are also considered masterpieces.

● Linking parts of sentences may involve:

1 putting related short pieces of information (e.g. dates or numbers) together, using **commas**:
   In 1941, at the age of 26, he …

2 putting related facts together to form one part of a sentence, using **parallel structures**:
   … he **directed and starred in** 'Citizen Kane' …
   ▸ See **33** *Parallel structures*.

3 joining parts of a sentence with **participles**:
   … 'Citizen Kane', **considered** by many people to be …
   ▸ See **34** *Participles*.

4 joining parts of a sentence with **relative clauses**:
   … a number of other films, **some of which are** considered …
   ▸ See **15** *Relative clauses*.

- Here is another example of a series of short sentences that should be linked:

Citizen Kane is about the life of a fictional newspaper owner. His name is Charles Foster Kane. The character is based on William Randolph Hearst. He was a US press baron. He was very famous at the time. He didn't like the film. He banned any mention of it in his newspapers. The story is told mostly through flashbacks. A reporter tries to find out why Kane's dying word is 'Rosebud'.

- The information can be linked as follows using relative clauses, commas, a parallel structure and a participle:

Citizen Kane is about the life of a fictional newspaper owner, whose name is Charles Foster Kane. The character is based on William Randolph Hearst, a US press baron who was very famous at the time. He didn't like the film and banned any mention of it in his newspapers. Told mostly through flashbacks, the film shows a reporter trying to find out why Kane's dying word is 'Rosebud'.

 Danger Zone

Focusing only on the information, not the presentation

Before you start writing, ask yourself these questions:

- *How can I group information/points in a longer sentence?*
- *How can I connect information/points within those longer sentences?*

When you have finished writing, be your own editor. Re-read and polish your sentences, particularly if you did not have time to do this when you were writing them.

Exercises

1 Turn these short sentences into one longer sentence by using relative and participle clauses and linking words. You may need to delete, add or move some words.

a The silent film era began in the late 19th century. It continued until the 1920s. Then recorded sound became possible.

b Politicians have become more and more reliant on focus groups. These came into existence in the 1990s. They involve groups of people giving their views on political issues. The people are carefully selected.

c Large hospitals can be cost-effective. They can move staff members to an area of greater need. These are staff members who have been underemployed in their part of the building.

d A small restaurant may have ambitions to expand. It can decide to make an offer on adjacent premises. This way it gains the additional space it requires.

e The research team was initially criticised for making slow progress. It was actually involved in a fundamental rethinking of domestic heating systems. This would lead to an innovative and successful design.

2 Using the same methods as in Exercise 1, use the short sentences below to create longer sentences (two sentences in each case).

a The Industrial Revolution transformed the entire world. It could be said to have started in Derbyshire and Shropshire. They are two counties in the north Midlands. Arkwright's Wheel was invented in Derbyshire in 1771. It used water power for the spinning of cotton. The Iron Bridge in Shropshire was built in 1781. It was the first arch bridge made of cast iron.

b Michael Cimino submitted a script for *Heaven's Gate* in 1971. When he submitted it to United Artists, it was called *The Johnson County War*. The project failed to attract high-profile actors. It was shelved for some time. The film finally began shooting in 1979. It had a budget of $11.6 million. In the end it cost $30 million.

Writing Tip

The ability to write successful long sentences is one of the key requirements of academic writing. If, when you are checking your writing, there seem to be too many short sentences, see if you can combine some of them into a single, more complex idea.

▶ **Look at these five ideas for part of an essay on the newspaper industry and think about how they could all be put together into one long sentence.**

1990s, arrival of internet	→	newspapers produced online versions	→	negative effect on sales of print papers	→	online version free	→	result: financial problems

- Focus first of all on the first and last points. This gives you an overall idea of the shape of your sentence. In this case, your sentence will begin with the arrival of the internet and end with a reference to a bad outcome (financial problems):
  arrival of internet → financial problems

 Remember!

When constructing a long sentence, always keep in mind how it is going to end, and build towards that ending.

- Now consider the points between the beginning and the end. The second point describes a response to the first point and the third point describes the result of that:
  1990s, arrival of internet → newspapers produced online versions → negative effect on sales of print papers

- These three points can be linked together to produce a coherent sentence that is long, but not too long.
  In the 1990s, newspapers **responded to** the arrival of the internet **by producing** online versions of their papers, **which had** a negative effect on sales of the print versions.

- Now consider the last two points. The last point describes the result of the fourth point:
  online version free → result: financial problems

- These two points can be linked together using the word 'since' to connect the cause and the result.
  Since the online version was free, the result was financial problems for those papers.
  Again, this is a perfectly good sentence on its own. However, the second sentence can be linked to the first using 'and' and a parallel structure: 'which had'..... (which) 'resulted in'.

- Here is the complete sentence, covering all five points:

In the 1990s, newspapers **responded to** the arrival of the internet **by producing** online versions of their papers, **which had** a negative effect on sales of the print versions **and**, **since** the online version was free, **resulted in** financial problems for those papers.

- Here is another example of how a successful long sentence can be built using linkers and a relative pronoun.

Online news: → welcomed by many, not necessarily by professional journalists → view of professional journalists: careers threatened → 'amateurs' willing to get little or no money

Online news has been welcomed by many, **but** not necessarily by established professional journalists, **who** see their careers threatened by people they regard as 'amateurs' **because** they are willing to supply articles for news and review websites for little or no money.

The sentence is a long one, consisting of four parts, but it has a coherent meaning as a whole because of the way the points are joined, presenting both a view on a particular subject and the reason for that view.

 Danger Zone

Losing control of long sentences

Keep re-reading your sentence as you are writing it. Make sure that each part of it relates to the other parts in a meaningful way.

> Political blogs are a good example of how online journalism can have a significant influence *even though only a small number of people read them, they are often key decision-makers and so* these blogs can have a serious impact on political debate. ✖

The beginning and end are fine and make a clear point, but the sentence becomes incoherent and ungrammatical in the middle.

> Political blogs are good examples of how online journalism can have a significant influence even though only a small number of people read them, because the people who do read them are often key decision-makers, and so these blogs can have a serious impact on political debate. ✔

Exercise

1 **In each case, write one long sentence that includes all of the points and information in the notes provided. You will need to use grammatical elements such as linkers, relative pronouns and parallel structures.**

a Sports psychology:
- based on belief many top competitors of similar ability
- winners/losers separated by state of mind
- also by ability to meet mental challenge not just physical one

b 1990s:
- significant in country's development
- economy grew faster than ever before
- number of social changes
- result: various problems

c Long-term storage of files:
- easy to access and requiring little storage space
- data is still present years or decades later
- danger: machine malfunction makes it unreadable
- problem: spare parts no longer available

39   Hedging (1): with verbs and adverbs

Unhedged claim:
Without staff consultation, organisational changes create as many problems as solutions.

Hedged claim:
Without staff consultation, organisational changes **tend to create** as many problems as solutions.

 **Writing Tip**

To ensure your credibility as a writer, be cautious when you are making a 'claim' (defined here as a statement that cannot be proven). The term often used for being cautious in this way is 'hedging', and this is a common feature of academic writing.

▶ Read this short text on energy use in offices and factories and look at the hedging language in bold.

Recent research by the Michael Case Foundation (2021) **seems to** confirm that factories and office buildings are responsible in the UK for 6% of energy consumption and 3% of carbon emissions. The report **suggests** that companies should prioritise the implementation of new policies to reduce these emissions. Such policies **often** involve adaptations to existing technology. Factories and offices are **typically** able to make these kinds of alterations without experiencing a reduction in their overall efficiency.

Using verbs to hedge

1   appear, seem, tend + to + verb; it appears/seems that...

For smaller organisations with limited resources, electronic storage **appears to reduce** costs.
Companies that have a purpose beyond profit **tend to be** more successful.
It seems that Creative Solutions failed to fulfil the two main demands of its client.

NOTE: The noun form of 'tend' can also be used: 'There is a tendency for successful companies to expand.' OR: 'Successful companies have a tendency to expand.'

2   can, could, may, might (modal verbs that express probability) + **verb**

An agreed change in the leadership of a team **can produce** thought-provoking results.
The slight fall in unemployment **might** improve consumer confidence.

NOTE: 'could' and 'might' are more cautious than 'can' and 'may'; and 'can' is the most common.

3   indicate, suggest that (more cautious than 'prove' or 'demonstrate')

Evidence **suggests that** low prices remain the key driver in consumer food choices.
The table below **indicates** that the UK events industry grew significantly from 2010 to 2020.

4   contribute to + noun phrase and **help to + verb**

Most commentators agree that deregulation **contributed to** the banking crisis of 2008.
An improvement in distribution channels **helps to reduce** the cost of a final product.

NOTE: These are less common hedging verbs. (Both suggest that the first thing is only partly responsible for the second.)

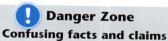

Danger Zone

Confusing facts and claims

Always consider whether you are stating a fact or making a claim.

Fact: Apple was founded as a company on 1 April 1976 in Cupertino, California.
Claim: (It seems that) the features of some Apple products should be reviewed.

Using adverbs to hedge

1 perhaps, possibly; probably (probability adverbs)

When to expand is **possibly** the most difficult decision a new business will make.

2 sometimes; normally, usually; frequently, often (frequency adverbs that hedge 'always')

Smaller shops **normally** suffer a decline in trade when a supermarket opens nearby.

3 hardly ever, occasionally, rarely, seldom (frequency adverbs that hedge 'never')

Flat organizational structures **rarely** offer good prospects for promotion.

Other hedging adverbs

apparently ('it appears to be like this')
This **apparently** minor incident caused an immediate loss in customer confidence.
arguably ('there may be some disagreement about this')
There are, **arguably**, five tests of a company's strength in its market.
relatively ('in comparison with other things')
Junior executives in the company will initially be assigned to **relatively** routine tasks.
typically ('as is the case with this type of person or thing')
Factories and offices are **typically** able to make these kinds of alterations …
generally ('usually true')
Carefully targeted staff development courses are **generally** effective.

Exercises

1 Rewrite these sentences using the verb (or a form of the verb) in brackets.

a The latest rise in unemployment will weaken consumer confidence in the economy. (*could*)
b Resistance to innovation comes from a fear of change. (*tend*)
c Smaller electronics companies were outperforming their larger rivals. (*seem*)
d Greater regulation of banking practice would enhance the reputation of the financial sector. (*help*)
e The evidence proves that stricter regulation of online loan companies is required. (*indicate*)
f Even 'scientific' decision-making is shaped by the personal values of the decision-maker. (*may*)
g The practice of 'short selling' brought about the collapse of Lehman Brothers. (*contribute*)

2 Choose the more appropriate adverb in each sentence.

a The process of 'deskilling' the workforce to allow for automation was (*arguably/seldom*) a consequence of the scientific management strategies applied during the early part of the 20th century.
b The senior management team (*relatively/apparently*) lost control of the company's strategic vision.
c Start-ups (*rarely/typically*) use major market research companies because they are small enough to approach customers directly for their views.
d The key component of an advertising campaign will (*probably/relatively*) be the message that a company wishes to convey to the potential customer.
e The elements of a person specification are (*arguably/normally*) split into 'essential' and 'desirable'.

40 Hedging (2): with adjectives and phrases

▶ Read this extract on a medical condition called epilepsy and look at the hedging language in bold.

The precise cause of epileptic seizures **is unlikely to** be established in the near future. Some researchers believe that the chance of developing epilepsy is, **to some extent**, genetic **in that** any person who starts having seizures has always had a genetic tendency to do so. **It could be argued that**, even if seizures start after a brain injury, this may be due to both a structural change and the person's genetic makeup.

Using adjectives to hedge

1 **It is possible/probable/likely/unlikely + 'that' clause**

> **It is possible that** high levels of stress at work will lead to illness.
> **It is unlikely that** medical research will determine the cause of autism in the near future.

2 **Noun phrase + is/are likely/unlikely to + verb**

> As Lemnick (2020) observes, government campaigns **are unlikely to have** any real impact on adult obesity.

Using 'it' + passive verb phrases

- for claims that may not be strong

> **It can/could be argued + 'that' clause**
> **It has been argued/suggested + 'that' clause**
> ... but **it is (or has been) claimed/said + 'that' clause**
> **It might be felt + 'that' clause**

> **It has been suggested that** schizophrenia should be regarded as a collection of disorders (More, 2016; Toms, 2018).

- for stronger claims

> **It is firmly believed/thought that** ...
> ... although **it is (widely/generally) accepted that** ...

> **It is generally accepted that** a positive mental attitude contributes to a patient's recovery (Cryer, 2019).

- for claims in specific contexts

> **It is reported + 'that' clause** (often used in reference to published reports)
> ... and **it is estimated + 'that' clause** (often used with statistics)

> **It is estimated that** five million Americans are currently living with Alzheimer's disease (Gibbs, 2021, p.82).

Improve Your Grammar

Phrases used to hedge

in some respects, to some extent (to place limits on a statement)
on balance (to give an opinion based on all the factors involved)
as a rule (usually but not always)
in principle (to say that something is theoretically possible)
in most/many cases and **the majority of** (to suggest that there are exceptions)
for the most part/on the whole/in general (generally true)

An independent consultant concluded that, **on balance**, the initial diagnosis was incomplete.
In most cases, medical practitioners argue that assisted suicide cannot be justified.
In principle, there is no reason why the same cloning techniques should not work on human cells.

Qualifying a statement

'Qualifying' something that you write means making the reader understand the particular way in which you think that it is true. It has a similar effect to hedging.

insofar as/to the extent that ('limiting' phrases used with clauses)
Lifestyle changes are effective **insofar as/to the extent that** they alleviate symptoms of the illness.

in the sense that/in that ('explanatory' phrases with clauses)
In the sense that/In that they block the function of bacterial cell walls, some of these new antibiotics offer new hope for long-term treatment.

in terms of/with *or* **in regard to** ('explanatory' phrases with noun phrases or gerunds)
The rehabilitation programme was unsuccessful **in terms of/with** *or* **in regard to** the targets set for improvement.

Exercises

1 Hedge or qualify these claims, using the words in brackets.

  a 80% of Quapaw Native Americans died from a smallpox virus introduced by European settlers. (*estimated*)
  b High levels of stress at work will lead to illness. (*likely to*)
  c Exercise is important; it may improve mental health. (*in that*)
  d Although it is still being trialled, this new antibiotic will have better long-term prospects. (*argued*)
  e The public health campaign was successful; it raised awareness of the issue. (*terms*)

2 Correct the mistakes in these hedged claims.

  a PFIs in the public health sector have suffered to extent from poor project management.
  b Restructuring these two hospitals will, on principle, improve their performance.
  c The treatment was successful insofar if it alleviated the symptoms.
  d It has claimed that people who live alone take longer to recover from some illnesses.
  e In the area of mental health, patients recover more quickly, as rule, if they receive counselling as well as medication.

3 Hedge this text, using language from this or the previous unit.

The latest research proves that poor diet is a major factor in a number of serious illnesses. The Government must therefore increase the amount of money it spends on education programmes. Improving the nation's diet will be cost-effective because it will reduce expenditure on the NHS. Fewer ill employees will also represent a significant saving to business by minimising the incidence of sick leave.

This sentence gives a definition of the term 'communications protocol'.

→

In computing, **a communications protocol** is the system of rules that allows computers to exchange messages.

 Writing Tip

It is often necessary to give a clear definition of a word or phrase you are using so that the reader knows exactly what you mean by it. Definitions should be given when you first use the particular term or phrase, and there are various approaches you can take.

Using category nouns and noun phrases to give a definition

- **The term** (the thing you are defining) + **be** + **category** (the wider group) + **a relative clause**:

  term　be　category　relative clause
  An optical fibre is a thin strand of glass that is designed to transmit light.

- Here is another example:

  term　be　category　relative clause
  Morse code is a form of communication that uses long and short sounds or flashes of light.

 Remember!

Don't leave out the category noun when you refer to the term for the first time:
A spectrograph separates an incoming wave into a frequency spectrum.
A spectrograph **is an instrument that** separates an incoming wave into a frequency spectrum. ✔

- The category nouns **means**, **method**, **process** and **technique** are often followed by **whereby** or **by which**:

Nonverbal communication is the **means by which/whereby** messages are conveyed visually rather than by words.

- The category nouns **device**, **implement**, **instrument**, **machine**, **mechanism** and **tool** are often followed by **for** + '**-ing**':

A transmitter is an electronic **device for producing** radio waves.

 Danger Zone
Not giving a proper definition

Your definition needs to be more than an example – it needs to provide an explanation.

A social networking site is an online platform such as Facebook, which has more than 800 million users. ✖
A social networking site is an online platform (such as Facebook) that seeks to bring people and their interests into contact with each other. ✔

Using different verbs to give a definition

Two groups of verbs are regularly used in definitions.

Describe, mean, refer to, signify

- Sentences with these verbs sometimes start with 'The term … ' or 'The word … ':

The term 'multiplexing' **describes** a process whereby several electronic signals are sent using only one connection.

Be defined as, be known as, be called

- If you are using a quotation or paraphrasing from a dictionary or another source, you can use **be** + **defined as**:

Lobbying **is defined** by Semeraro **as** the attempt to influence the policy decisions of legislators or government agencies.

- If you are making your own definition, use **can/could/may/might** + **be** + **defined as**:

Propaganda **could be defined as** a form of communication that tries to influence the views of a community through biased information.

NOTE: If you intend to define something in a specific way, you can write: 'In this essay I will define X as Y'.

- Use **be** + **known as** and **be** + **called** when you put the term at the end of the sentence:

A collection of people who come together to seek to influence public policy **is known as/is called** an advocacy group.

 Remember!

You can give a short definition within a longer sentence by using brackets:
Every studio contains at least one isolation booth (a small room with extra soundproofing).

Exercises

1 Improve or correct these definitions.

a An avatar can be defined by Spinrad in *Songs from the Stars* (1980) as a representation of a human that allows him or her to participate in a virtual world.
b A digital immigrant is a person was born before the start of the digital age.
c Data mining is a process which a company develops profiles of potential customers through information collated from their online behaviour.
d A computer virus is a program such as the Conficker worm, which attacked British and French defence systems in 2008.
e Apple Inc. produces and sells consumer electronics, personal computers and computer software.
f A mouse is a process for controlling the movement of a cursor on a computer screen.

2 Write definitions of these terms in your own words.

a Cyber bullying
b Wikipedia
c Globalisation
d A USB flash drive
e A chat room

42 Introducing an example

For some time now, there has been considerable discussion about modern farming methods. The debate over the use of pesticides is **just one example**.

Writing Tip

When introducing an example, it is important to make a clear and accurate link between your main argument or claim and the information you are using to support it.

▶ Read this sentence from a report on modern farming methods.

Government control affects many areas of farming and farmers often suffer as a result: e.g. farm management. ✖

What's wrong: The example is not clearly linked to the main argument and it has been incorporated into the sentence in an ungrammatical way.

● Here is the same sentence with the example clearly and accurately integrated:

Government control affects many areas of farming and farmers often suffer as a result. **An example of this can be seen** in the current approaches to farm management. ✔

Ways of introducing examples

1 Using the word 'example'

The general public have had a significant impact on farming practice. **A good example of this is** the pressure that has been mounted over the decades to minimise the battery farming of chickens.

2 Using the phrases 'for example' or 'for instance'

There are factors other than the weather that affect the livelihood of farmers. **For example/For instance**, government policies are also highly influential.

3 Using 'such as' (particularly for lists)

Many factors, **such as** the weather, government policy and public demand, affect the way farms are run.

4 Using phrases connected with the verbs 'illustrate' and 'exemplify'

Disagreement over the meaning of 'sustainable agriculture' **is illustrated/exemplified by** the difference between the Government's definition of it and that of many farmers.

Remember!

The language that you use to speak can be very different from the language that you use to write. Expressions such as *like, you know* and *I mean*, which are informal expressions often used to give examples, should never be used for this purpose in written work.

▶ Here are some more examples of where to use these phrases in a sentence. Compare them with the sentences above.

There are many farming myths. **Take, for example,** organic farming, which is supposed to be more environmentally friendly. Many people would argue …

Public pressure **is just one example of** the many forces that can be exerted on farming practice.

Just one event can destroy a harvest – a severe tropical storm, **for instance**.

An illustration of the type of misinformation that reaches the public domain is the insistence that small-scale farming is less productive than large-scale farming.

Danger Zone

Confusing 'e.g.' and 'i.e.'

E.g. and **i.e.** are abbreviations of Latin terms.
E.g. (*exempli gratia*) means 'for example'; **i.e.** (*id est*) means 'that is'.

▶ **Look at this sentence:**

Types of farming (e.g. crop rotation and monoculture) will be compared.

This means that many types of farming will be compared; crop rotation and monoculture are examples.

▶ **Now look at this sentence:**

The types of farming in the region (i.e. crop rotation and monoculture) will be compared.

This means that crop rotation and monoculture are the only types of farming in the region. The abbreviation 'i.e.' is used for defining what has been mentioned before. Do not use it for giving examples.

NOTE: Some tutors may prefer you not to use these abbreviations. Check whether your tutor or university has a policy on their use.

Exercises

1 Underline the information that is being exemplified.

a **An illustration of** just how difficult it can be to pump groundwater can be seen in some coastal areas, where development has been complicated by the contamination of seawater.
b A range of educational activities can take place on farms, which may even boost income. **Examples of these** can be seen across the country in the 'farm visits' that have been set up for schoolchildren.
c The increasing population has led to growth in agriculture but this has resulted in a number of complications. The destruction of animal habitats **is one example**.
d Many laws are designed to protect waterways and land from degradation; **for example**, the Water Resources Act of 1991, which carries a substantial fine for water pollution.
e Technology has taken over many traditional approaches to enhancing crop performance, **such as** the monitoring of weed growth and irrigation systems.

2 Decide whether or not these sentences are correct, and correct those that are not.

a This can improve many people's quality of life like by enabling them to have a better diet.
b Some developing countries (i.e. in South America and Africa) rely heavily on income from farming.
c Some statistics on organic farming can be surprising, for example, sugar cane.
d The decision to expand coffee-growing regions was an illustration of the impact of consumer demand on agricultural decision-making.

3 Insert the missing words.

a Australia is an .... of a country that has vast areas of organic farmland.
b There have been many changes in agricultural practice. ...., for example, the huge increase in organic agricultural land over the past decade.
c Some crops, ... as cereals, are more widely grown than others around the globe.
d The public's desire to purchase fresh produce is clearly .... by the growing support for small-scale farms and their produce.
e .... example of a tried-and-trusted piece of farm equipment is the tractor.

Writing Tip

Citations that are accurately incorporated into your writing strengthen your arguments and significantly enhance the overall impact of what you say.

Sources that are referred to in a piece of writing must be **cited** in an appropriate way, using correct grammar.

 Remember!

Your university may require you to use a particular system for incorporating citations. It is advisable to check this out. In this unit we use the Harvard system, but note that there are variations within this system.

▶ Look at the source below, and the student's sentence on the topic of child development.

Source

Despite the existence of pre-school education and the efforts that working parents put into finding the 'best' schools for their children, <u>the family home has the greatest impact on educational development</u>. This can clearly be seen when you look at the studies …

Child Development, Rogers and Green, 2008

Student

Rogers and Green (2008) quote:

'the family home has the greatest

impact on educational development'.

What's wrong: The citation has been incorporated into the sentence in an ungrammatical way.

● Here are some correct ways of incorporating citations:

1 Author(s) + date in brackets + verb (e.g. *argue, point out, state, suggest, insist, assert*) **+ that**:

Rogers and Green (2020) argue that 'the family home has the greatest impact on educational development'.

2 As + author(s) + date in brackets + verb (e.g. *state, show, demonstrate, point out*) **+ colon** + quote:

As Rogers and Green (2020) point out: 'the family home has the greatest impact on educational development'.

3 According to + author(s) + date in brackets + comma + quote:

According to Rogers and Green (2020), 'the family home has the greatest impact on educational development'.

4 By mentioning the source first:

In their book, *Child Development* **(2020), Rogers and Green state that** 'the family home has the greatest impact on educational development'.

5 By rephrasing the view and adding the author(s) + date in brackets at the end of the sentence:

Children's educational progress is most influenced by their home life **(Rogers and Green, 2020).**

▸ See **44** *Paraphrasing*.

- Here are some more examples of citations. Compare them with the examples above.

In his famous book *Circle Game*, Minton (2019) drew attention to the need for 'specialised centres'.
As Peacock and Tramer argue: 'nothing holds back a child more than inattention'.
Klein, in his paper 'Nothing to Lose' (2005), gives an example of a successful classroom exercise.
The method lost credibility when parents noticed signs of regression in their children (Packam, 2004).
Thomas *et al.* (2017) dismiss this theory, stating that 'studies consistently show that the logic is flawed'.
Like many earlier experts, Quimper is of the view that 'childhood is our only stage of innocence'.

▶ See 'Quoting' in **24** *Inverted commas*.

Tenses in citations

- When the citation is being used to support a current view or your own view, the **present simple** tense and the **present perfect** tense are most commonly used:
  Thomas *et al.* (2019) **clearly identify** the areas of need. As they rightly **state**, these are 'on our own doorstep'.
  Experiments by Greenstein *et al.* (2019, 2020) **have demonstrated** the importance of interactive play.

- You can use the **past simple** tense to refer back to a past source that was important at the time:
  Capstan (1965) **defined** the activity as a 'two-tiered initiative', a term that is still used today.
  Jo and Singh (2007) **conducted** a key experiment on identical twins in 2001.

 **Danger Zone**
More than one author/publication

When more than one publication is cited, use a semicolon to separate them.
(Sacha, 2016 and Denver, 2017) ✗   (Sacha, 2016; Denver, 2017) ✓

When four or more authors produced one work, use the term '*et al.*' in italics after the first author of the publication and use a plural reporting verb:
(Burke *et al.*, 2010) ✓   Rainer *et al.* (2004) argue that ✓

Exercises

1 **Decide whether these citations have been introduced into each sentence correctly. Correct those that are wrong.**
  a As Jennings states that 'The home is of paramount importance.'
  b No one really knew what term to use, until Mo (1995) comes up with the expression, 'blue hour'.
  c Special Educational Needs, as Pil and Grew (2017) note, is a growing area of concern.
  d Barton (2018) quotes that few people really understand the problem.
  e Green *et al.* argues that price is always a factor.
  f According to Nudrun *et al.* (2018), television can be a useful educational tool.
  g In his paper, 'Giving and Receiving' (2016), Jameson explains his theory.
  h According to Pine-Smith (2005) argues, 'we have to take into account the child's home environment'.

2 **Correct the punctuation in these citations. Two sentences are correct.**
  a Given sufficient support, children thrive in school (Kinnock and Peters, 2017).
  b Compliance is a critical factor (Peters 2013 and Lilley 1999).
  c This behaviour has been examined in a number of works (Johnson, 1996; Coates, 1998; Green, 2005; Kitty, 2017).
  d While nobody can challenge this idea, 'other areas of a child's life also play their part (Fielding 2004).'
  e Grahams (2019) insists that 'this old notion has to be rejected once and for all.

44 Paraphrasing

Paraphrasing involves rewriting someone else's words using your own words. You need to combine various paraphrasing techniques in order to do this effectively.

 Writing Tip

A good paraphrase:
- is a useful alternative to a direct quotation
- shows that you understand the original text
- is normally approximately the same length as the original text
- always acknowledges the source.

Using synonyms (words with the same meaning)

▶ Read this original or 'source' text and think about which words could be replaced by synonyms.

> Soller (2018) states: 'Companies that show a genuine interest in charitable activities can earn the respect of the buying public.'

 Remember!

You don't need to change:
- very common words that have no alternatives, e.g. 'television' or 'university'
- specialised words from particular subject areas, e.g. 'limited company' or 'diagnosis'.

- Here is a version of the source text, using synonyms:

  Businesses that **demonstrate** a **real** interest in charitable activities can **gain** the respect of **consumers**, according to Soller (2018).

  NOTE: An ordinary dictionary, a dictionary of synonyms or a thesaurus will help you find synonyms.

Changing the form of words

▶ Read this source text and think about how the form of the underlined words could be changed.

> Michaels (2019) states: 'Some charities owe their <u>success</u> to the <u>selective</u> use of consultants.'

- Here is a version of the source text, changing the noun 'success' into the adjective 'successful', and the adjective 'selective' into the adverb 'selectively'.

  Michaels (2019) states that some charities are **successful** because they use consultants **selectively**.

Changing the grammatical structure

▶ Read this source text and think of a different comparative structure to paraphrase the underlined section.

> Polson (2020) states: 'Persuading the public to sign up to monthly donations is a <u>more cost-effective policy than</u> collecting single contributions.'

- Here is a version of the source text, using a different grammatical structure:

  Collecting single contributions is **not as cost-effective as** persuading the public to sign up to monthly donations, according to Polson (2020).

- Other grammatical changes when paraphrasing could include:

Active ↔ passive

The Government offered charities a tax break. → Charities were offered a tax break.

Despite ↔ although

Despite offering charities a tax break, the Government … → Although the Government had offered …

Cause ↔ effect

Tax breaks led to increased revenue. → Charities increased their revenue as a result of …

Modal verb ↔ adjective

Charities can increase their revenue … → It is possible for charities to increase their revenue …

Verb ↔ participle

Before they introduced the tax breaks … → Before introducing the tax breaks …

Using all three approaches

▶ Read this source text and think about how it could be paraphrased.

> Gates (2019): 'Indirect delivery via institutions such as the World Bank may mean that UK charity contributions are lost to corrupt practices.'

- Here are some changes that can be made:
  - start with the **effect** (funds disappearing) rather than the cause
  - change the **word forms** (e.g. corrupt practices → corruption)
  - use **synonyms** (e.g. via → through; institutions → organisations)
  - change a **grammatical structure** (e.g. are lost → could disappear)

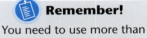 **Remember!**
You need to use more than one of these techniques to produce a full paraphrase.

- Here is a paraphrase of the source text, with the above changes:

Gates (2019) argues that British aid funds could disappear through corruption if they are distributed indirectly through organisations such as the World Bank.

Exercises

1 Replace the underlined words with synonyms.

  a Aid workers <u>need to</u> have a degree of <u>tolerance</u> towards cultural differences.
  b Human rights charities <u>censured</u> the <u>harsh</u> treatment of prisoners by the regime.
  c <u>Laws</u> to <u>prevent</u> bogus charities from operating were <u>wholeheartedly</u> welcomed.
  d The two charities worked <u>tirelessly</u> against the <u>damaging</u> effects of child labour.

2 Rewrite these sentences following the instructions in brackets.

  a The report advised the charity to extend the range of its projects. (*Use 'extensive'.*)
  b An excess of disaster campaigns can lead to 'compassion fatigue'. (*Start with 'Compassion fatigue …'.*)
  c Familiarity with local customs is essential for aid workers. (*Use 'familiar'.*)
  d Although it raised enough money, FoodAid could not get supplies to the region. (*Use 'despite' and 'unable'.*)

3 Write paraphrases of these texts.

  a Myers (2019) states: 'A successful aid advertisement needs to combine the elicitation of compassion with serious factual information about the state of play on the ground.'
  b Davis (2021) states: 'It is likely that the Government will ring-fence its expenditure on foreign aid, whatever the pressure of its deficit-cutting programme.'
  c Briggs (2011) states: 'Competition amongst charities has never been greater than it is at the moment.'

45 Incorporating data

During your studies, you will come across various types of **data** in a range of formats. Here are some examples:

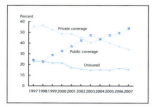 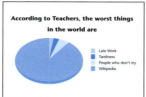 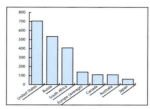 

 Writing Tip

Whether you are reporting your own data or using a source, the information must be clearly and accurately incorporated into your writing, using appropriate vocabulary.

▶ **Read this paragraph from an essay about research into shopping habits and think about how the vocabulary could be improved.**

> The study, performed by a marketing research team, was created to find out information about people's buying habits. A general group of approximately 100 shoppers were interviewed over a four-week period. During this time a lot of data was assembled and checked. Prior to the study, the research team had thought that there would be many differences in the subjects' approach to purchasing. The results showed they were right. They discovered that men spent much more time than women researching their purchases on the internet. However, women shopped more often and spent more overall. These results are the same as those of other similar studies.

What's wrong: The vocabulary is not precise enough. There are certain words and phrases that are commonly used to describe data and few of them have been used.

● Here are some guidelines for describing data:

1 Use appropriate verbs and verb forms

> The study, **conducted** by a marketing research team, was **designed** to **gather** information about people's buying habits.

2 Use appropriate nouns and noun phrases

> The team interviewed a **random selection** of 100 **participants** over a four-week period.

3 Use appropriate adjectives and adverbs to give a more accurate description

> Prior to the study, the consultants had predicted that there would be **considerable variation** in the subjects' approach to purchasing. They found that men spent **significantly** more time than women researching their purchases on the internet.

4 Use appropriate phrases to compare data

> However, women shopped **more frequently** and spent **larger sums of money** overall.

▸ See **16** *Comparing and contrasting* and **17** *Describing similarities and differences*.

5 Use correct prepositions with nouns, verbs and adjectives

> These findings are **consistent with** those of other similar studies.

▸ See **50** and **51** *Using prepositions*.

• Here are some more examples of vocabulary commonly used to describe data:

The experiment was **set up** in a secure environment.
The **main aim** of the study was to **investigate** buying habits.
The study **focused on** people aged 20–30.
A range of **variables** had to be considered.
The researchers were looking for **evidence** to prove their **theory**.
Spending **varied** each day but sometimes **reached** very high **levels**.
One group purchased **a greater number** of items than the other.
A number of **significant differences** were found.
The **researchers** made some interesting **observations**.
The findings **suggest/indicate/show** that …
Results have **revealed** a number of **significant differences**.
Certain **conclusions** can be **drawn** from the **figures**.
Other findings were **inconclusive**.

 Remember!
Write numbers from one to ten in words (e.g. eight) and numbers above ten in numerals (e.g. 88). Percent can be written as one word or two (per cent).

 Danger Zone

Number and amount

'Number' is usually used with countable nouns that have a plural form, such as *man/men*; and *item/items*. 'Amount' is usually used with uncountable nouns that have only one form, such as *evidence* and *information*.

a significant amount of people ✗   the number of researches ✗
a significant number of people ✔   the amount of research ✔

Exercises

1 Choose the more appropriate option in italics.

a Trials were *conducted/designed* over a two-week period.
b The data was carefully *explored/analysed*.
c A number of *variables/differences* between the groups were evident.
d The data revealed some *significant/main* differences.
e Purchasing patterns were *consistent/the same* across the age groups.
f Consumerism has *gained/reached* an all-time high in some cities.

2 Complete each gap with an appropriate word from the box.

| results   participants   finding   aim   conducted   observations   difference   predicted   variation |

A hundred (a) ……….. were involved in a study designed and (b) ……….. by a group of head teachers. The (c) ……….. of the study was to compare the reading ability of students across the secondary-school years. The teachers (d) ……….. that the study would show a considerable (e) ……….. between boys' and girls' reading scores in years seven to nine. After that they expected less (f) ……….. .
Their (g) ……….. were inconclusive. However, during the course of the study, they made a number of interesting (h) ……….. . One of these suggests that schools would do well to encourage boys to read newspapers, rather than books – a (i) ……….. they intend to research further.

Doctors use electrocardiograms <u>and that sort of thing</u> to investigate heart problems. → Doctors use **tests such as** electrocardiograms to investigate heart problems.

 Writing Tip

The kind of language you might use in conversation is often inappropriate in academic work because it is too informal or imprecise. In your written work, you need to develop a precise, objective style and to avoid colloquial language, such as slang and clichés.

Words and phrases to avoid

▶ Read the following sentences and think about which words you would avoid in formal writing, and how you might replace them.

1 It would be dead easy for the Government to make unhealthy foods much more expensive. ✗
2 There are loads of examples of advertising campaigns that have changed public attitudes to health. ✗
3 Gone are the days when the public would automatically pay attention to a ministerial broadcast. ✗
4 The town-centre workshops were brilliant. ✗

What's wrong

Sentences using formal language

1 Colloquial or slang terms such as *dead easy, cool, cute, kids, guys, ad, uni* should be avoided in formal writing. → It would be **relatively straightforward** for the Government to make unhealthy foods much more expensive. ✓

2 Conversational language such as *loads of, a bit, a couple of, a lot of, sort of* and *stuff* should also be avoided. → There are **numerous** examples of advertising campaigns that have changed public attitudes to health. ✓

3 *Gone are the days when; to turn a blind eye; crystal clear; at the end of the day; to stick out like a sore thumb*: these are all examples of clichés that should be avoided. → **The era has passed when** the public would automatically pay attention to a ministerial broadcast. ✓

4 Expressions such as *brilliant, really good/bad, appalling* and *disgusting* should be replaced with more objective or restrained terms. → The town-centre workshops were **highly effective**. ✓

Using *it* … and *there* …

- 'I' and 'we' are often avoided in academic English by using impersonal structures such as *It* … and *there* …

- In the structure **It + verb + 'that' clause**, you can use 'it' as an impersonal subject for your sentence:

I believe that local authorities should offer more incentives to people who might be considering cycling to work. → **It could be argued** that local authorities should offer more incentives to people who might be considering cycling to work.

- In the structure **There + verb + noun phrase**, you can use *there* to introduce your idea:

We can all understand why people enjoy driving their own cars. → **There are a number of reasons** why people enjoy driving their own cars.

- Here are some more examples:

It seems clear that the public now recognise the link between exercise and health.
There can be little doubt that children are influenced by what they see on television.

When to use *I* and *we*

There are times when it can be appropriate to use these pronouns in formal writing.

- 'I' (or 'we' if you are working in a group) can be used when you are describing the scope of your argument:
  In the conclusion, **I** will make some recommendations for encouraging children to eat healthier food.
  ◗ See **48** *The language of argument.*

- 'I' (often with *would*) can be used to clarify your position during an essay. Useful verbs include *accept, argue, consider, propose, suggest*:
  I would accept, however, that this argument has not yet been won.

- 'We' can be used when you are writing about society in general:
  Unless **we** take positive action, children who are growing up today will face the avoidable medical conditions that result from overeating.

 **Remember!**

You can use words such as *essay, evidence, research* and *statistics* as the subjects of your sentences to give a more impersonal tone: e.g.:
This essay will discuss ...; Research has shown that ...; Statistics suggest that ...

Exercises

1 Amend the sentences, to avoid colloquial or slang terms.

  a One ad in a successful campaign shows a young dad in a park, who is looking after a couple of kids, and who fails to notice some of the dangers present in the situation.
  b In the promotion of their food products, some companies turn a blind eye to the health risks for children.
  c Encouraging young people to think that it is cool to become drunk is disgusting.
  d If young people suspect that they are being patronised, they may avoid the campaign message like the plague.
  e The problem of overeating won't be sorted by health campaigns on their own.

2 Rewrite these sentences, using *it* or *there* rather than *I* or *we*.

  a I think that food and drink advertisements that target children under ten should be banned.
  b We have to recognise that a car can play an important role in a person's sense of autonomy.
  c I believe in the food industry regulating itself in the area of advertising, rather than in creating new laws.
  d We have seen a demand among consumers for information about the food and drink that they purchase.
  e I am convinced that young people are now much more aware of the dangers of alcohol abuse.

Writing Tip

In your written work, your tutors will expect grammar and vocabulary that is appropriate to an academic style. There are various structures and techniques you can use to achieve this, many of which have been covered in this book.

Formal grammar

- Using **relative clauses** to convey additional information:

The Democratic Republic of the Congo is Africa's second largest country. It used to be a Belgian colony. → The Democratic Republic of the Congo, **which used to be a Belgian colony**, is Africa's second largest country.

▶ See **15** *Relative clauses*.

- Building sentences around **nouns** rather than verbs or adjectives:

It is easy to understand why the country objected at first to having peacekeeping forces within its borders. → The country's initial **objection** to peacekeeping forces within its borders is understandable.

▶ See **18** *Using noun phrases*.

- Using **the passive** for a style that focuses on an event rather than a person or people:

Officials set up polling stations in every community across the region. → Polling stations **were set up** in every community across the region.

▶ See **7** *Using the passive*.

- Using **a single complex word** instead of a phrase:

People began to lose their faith in the new Government when it stopped people from leaving their houses after dusk. → **Disillusionment** with the new Government set in when a dusk **curfew** was imposed.

▶ See **52** *Creating longer words* and **53** *Using single words for impact*.

- Using **sophisticated linkers** rather than simple ones:

The situation continued to be unstable, but people queued all day at the polling stations. → **Despite** the instability of the situation, people queued all day at the polling stations.

▶ See **26**, **27**, **28** and **29** *Linking*.

- Using words and techniques to make **different parts** of your writing **fit together** in a more formal way:

Kasa-Vubu, who was President of the Congo, and Lumumba, who was the Prime Minister, adopted significantly different approaches to the country's relationship with Belgium. → Kasa-Vubu and Lumumba, President and Prime Minister of the Congo **respectively**, adopted significantly different approaches to the country's relationship with Belgium.

▶ See **30** *Signposting*, **31** *Using pronouns correctly* and **32** *Avoiding repetition of words*.

Formal vocabulary

- The use of more complex vocabulary will enhance the formality of your writing. Here are some examples:

The situation ~~got worse~~ **deteriorated**, however, prior to the elections.
There was ~~very large~~ **overwhelming** support for a change of government.
~~Not many~~ **Few** citizens at the time were surprised by the ~~large~~ **significant** turnout at the election.
The newly elected party realised that social inequality was the first issue they had to ~~deal with~~ **address**.
The opposition was keen to ~~show~~ **demonstrate** its distrust in the election process.
Errors in the electoral process were described by the regime as ~~very small~~ **negligible**.

- Some Latin phrases are common in formal, academic writing:
For many citizens **the status quo** (the existing situation) was no longer acceptable.

Other Latin phrases include:

bona fide (genuine):
Voters doubted that the building was a bona fide polling station.

de facto (existing, but not officially agreed):
It may be necessary to negotiate with a de facto government until an internationally accepted administration is established.

per capita (per head/for each person):
The GDP per capita in the region is estimated to be $600.

pro rata (in proportion):
By inviting opposition politicians into his Cabinet, the Prime Minister accepted a pro rata loss in his party's overall power.

vice versa (reversing the order of two things just mentioned):
The economic situation often determines political decisions, rather than vice versa.

 Remember!
Some tutors may prefer you not to use Latin terms. Check whether your department has a policy on their use.

Exercises

1 Rewrite the sentences, following the instructions in brackets.

a An enquiry has been initiated into voting irregularities. The irregularities seemed to have occurred in the north of the region. (*Combine the sentences using 'that'.*)

b The President spoke briefly with the leader of the majority party, before the leader was pronounced Prime Minister. (*Use the words 'consultation' and 'latter'.*)

c The governing party enacted a series of laws to grant religious freedom to the population. (*Start with 'A series …' and leave out 'the governing party'.*)

d Monitors had to ensure that all the adults in the region could get to polling stations. (*Use 'accessible'.*)

2 Replace the underlined text with a more formal word or Latin phrase.

a The Prime Minister successfully <u>dealt with</u> the major problems facing the country's infrastructure.

b There were <u>not a lot of</u> objections to the introduction of new voting regulations.

c An <u>unofficial</u> leader has emerged from the ranks of the rebel army.

d Steyn argues that in the process of nation building, capitalism promotes political freedom and <u>the same applies the other way round.</u>

e A lack of electricity means that factory workers can only be employed for half the day, resulting in a <u>proportionate</u> reduction in their wages.

Writing Tip

This unit presents some examples of the language you can use for each part of an essay. When you are planning your next assignment, highlight some of the words and phrases in this unit that you could use.

Essay title

To what extent has the fair trade movement been a success?

→ In order to address this question successfully, you need to use an acceptable, academic style of language.

Stating the scope

▶ Read this introduction to an essay on 'fair trade' and think about the function of the words in bold.

First, this essay will **define** the term 'fair trade' and **describe** in brief the history of the movement. **Then** it will **consider** three cases where fair-trade initiatives have benefited communities in the developing world, and **examine** with statistical evidence how general these benefits have been. **Next**, it will **move on to** criticisms of the movement, **analysing** two important concerns that have been raised in the last five years. It will **conclude** by making a recommendation for the future of the scheme.

● Stating the scope of your essay normally involves verbs such as: analyse, consider, define, examine; and sequencing language such as: first, in the second part/half, next, then, finally, start, move on to, follow, finish, conclude.

Your thesis statement

● Your department may require a 'thesis statement', summarising your point of view in one sentence near the beginning of your essay. Thesis statements often use the modal verbs should, will, can and ought to, and sometimes connectors such as however, although or despite/in spite of.

I will argue that the fair-trade movement, **despite** some of its failures, **should** be supported and improved.

Supporting your claims

● You should make clear that the claims and views you express are supported by concrete evidence, and not simply personal opinions that you cannot back up. The phrases below are more appropriate than expressions such as 'I think', 'the way I see it' or 'I do not agree':

It can be argued that …
(On balance), it seems that …
▶ See **39** and **40** *Hedging*.

 Remember!

If there is evidence to support your view, you should refer to it. Otherwise your view will lose impact or raise unanswered questions in the reader's mind.

● You can direct your reader by highlighting your main arguments and using signposting language:

The first point to be made is that …
The latter argument is flawed because …
▶ See **30** *Signposting*.

● To support your views, you can refer to research:

Research demonstrates that …
Studies have shown that …
▶ See **43** *Citing* and **44** *Paraphrasing*.

- You can also provide examples to illustrate your arguments:
  A good example of this is …/Such a situation is evident when …
  ◆ See **42** *Introducing an example.*

Commenting on counter-arguments

- To provide a balanced viewpoint, you may wish to comment on opposing arguments:

> **Despite** these successes, there is an argument that very little financial benefit actually reaches farmers in the producer countries (Griffiths, 2010). This is a claim which is difficult to prove, **however**, due to a lack of formal research into the impact of fair trade measures in developing countries.

- You can signal this by using connectors that express contrast such as: although, but, despite, however or while.
  ◆ See **26** *Linking: contrasting.*

- You can introduce other counter-arguments using this structure:
  Another/a second etc./a further argument against fair trade is that …
  Another/a second etc./a further objection to fair trade is that …

Drawing conclusions and making recommendations

- To introduce a conclusion, you can use a fixed expression such as:

To conclude, …	In conclusion, …	To sum up, …	Clearly, therefore, …
To summarise, …	In summary, …	As we have seen, …	On balance, …

  or you can begin a clause:
  We can say therefore that …/It can be said that …
  Thus, we can conclude that …/it can therefore be concluded that …
  On the basis of these arguments, we can conclude that …/it can be concluded that …

- To make a recommendation, you can use an introductory phrase such as:
  On the basis of these arguments, it would be advisable (for someone/something) to + verb …
  It follows that there is a (pressing/urgent) need (for someone/something) to + verb …
  or you can use a sentence ending in the passive form:
  … should/must be done/carried out.
  … is (therefore) recommended/needed.
  … could/should be considered.

> **To conclude**, given that more than fifty years have passed since the slogan 'Trade not aid' was adopted at the United Nations Conference on Trade and Development in Delhi, **it seems clear that** an independent formal impact study with access to all the relevant data **should be carried out**.

Exercise

You are answering the question 'Globalisation has as many casualties as success stories'. Use the essay outline below to write a paragraph stating the scope of your essay.

a Definition of globalisation
b Drawbacks of globalisation in developing countries
c Loss of cultural identity
d Political gains
e Recent success of some global campaigns
f Conclusion: benefits outweigh disadvantages

49   The language of critique

 Writing Tip

'To criticise' is to say what you think is wrong about something; 'to critique' is to offer a more detailed examination of a topic that may make positive as well as negative comments.

You will not necessarily agree with all the arguments that are put forward on topics, and experts may also disagree amongst themselves. In order to present a balanced view when you write, you will need to discuss areas of disagreement (as well as agreement), using appropriate academic language.

▶ Read this short paragraph on behaviourism and look at the language in bold.

Despite his **pioneering** work at Harvard University from 1958 to 1974, a **weakness with** Skinner's ideas on human behaviour is that they may be overly **reductive**. An early and **influential** critique of Skinner's work on verbal behaviour by Chomsky (1959), for example, **casts doubt** on the notion that adult language use can be described purely, or even helpfully, in terms of responses or behaviours.

Adjectives (grouped by meaning) **for expressing your own positive and negative views**

admirable	excellent, exemplary, first-rate, impressive, outstanding	unimpressive
important	notable, significant, valuable	minor, inconsequential
original	innovative, influential, pioneering, seminal, ground-breaking	unoriginal
helpful	informative, illuminating, instructive, useful	unhelpful
clear	coherent, logical, systematic	inconsistent
detailed	exhaustive, meticulous, rigorous, thorough, comprehensive	incomplete, reductive
compelling	convincing, persuasive, plausible, valid	unconvincing
accurate	appropriate, precise, clear-cut	flawed

Pim makes a **convincing** case that two types of psychosis may result from childhood abuse.
The second report gives an **illuminating** and **detailed** overview of the concept of motivation.
Gray's study of animal behaviour seems **incomplete** in terms of its selection process.

NOTE: Some adverbs can also convey a positive position, e.g.: 'Bosun clearly establishes/writes convincingly/examines thoroughly …'

 Danger Zone
Being overly critical

While some negative adjectives are useful, critical arguments are more frequently expressed using a negative structure or by drawing a comparison using 'less' + a positive adjective:

The view put forward by Homan seems **less helpful/impressive/convincing** than that of Seager.
Arguably, the research conducted by Jaggard and his team was **less rigorous** because …

Verbs for commenting on other writers' views

Positive verbs	acknowledge, celebrate, confirm, corroborate, praise, substantiate, support, uphold, validate, verify
Negative verbs	accuse, be critical of, cast doubt on, challenge, contest, criticise, disagree with, question, refute, take issue with

Adler's contribution to the discipline of counselling must be **acknowledged**.
Recent research has **corroborated** Zimbardo's early outstanding studies.
Holmes (2007), however, **takes issue with** Pitt's view of Gestalt psychology.

Structures for presenting your own negative views

1 A/The drawback/problem/weakness with X's/this argument/method/theory *etc.* + be (+ noun phrase/that)

A problem with this theory is that it fails to take full account of impulsive behaviour.
A weakness with (or 'in') **both of these therapies is** the difficulty in evaluating their success.

2 X's/This argument/analysis etc. overlooks/fails to account for *etc.* + noun phrase

Mellor's interpretation overlooks the recent research undertaken by Cross and Ingrams.
This approach fails to account for behavioural change in later adolescence.

3 The report/research *etc.* would have been/would be more interesting/relevant *etc.* if …

The report would have been more interesting if it had included a section on childhood behaviour.
The findings might have been more persuasive if the sample group had been larger.

 Remember!

You can make your negative views more cautious by using words like 'perhaps', 'tends' and 'might,' as you can see in the last example in each of the three sections above.

▶ See **39** and **40** *Hedging (1) and (2)*.

Exercises

1 Add one word to each sentence to make it correct.

a Harry Harlow was criticised using rhesus macaque monkeys in his isolation experiments.
b Another problem the case study method is that it is susceptible to researcher bias.
c The proposed review might be more instructive it referred to Popper's criticism of psychoanalysis.
d Dewey is praised Forster for integrating psychology with social issues.
e The notion that free will is an illusion challenged in Gray's article.
f The study would been more illuminating if it had taken social settings into account.

2 Correct each sentence by adding one of these words/phrases: *to overlook, the claim that, a ground-breaking, make a systematic, innovative in, supports, question the*

a Beck (1994) the view that CBT has been effective for treating depression.
b Piaget (1936) was the first psychologist to study of cognitive development.
c Klein was both her techniques and her theories on infant development.
d Titchener created psychology programme at Cornell University.
e Bloch upholds Watzlawick's insights into communication were revolutionary.
f Sturges and Briony idea that subjective experiences are the only way to study human behaviour.
g Lemchok's work appears the distinction between competence and performance.

50   Using prepositions (1)

Prepositions complete phrases or form a relationship between words in a sentence.
Common prepositions include: at, of, in, on, for, off, out of, from, by, with, without.
Other prepositions include: as, beyond, against, throughout, between, concerning, towards.

 Writing Tip

Prepositions are widely used in English, but unfortunately there are few rules for their use. Good writers learn combinations of words and prepositions that are relevant to their subjects.

▶ Here are some features of prepositions:

- They can be used to indicate time, movement, place, etc. in both concrete and abstract ways:
  over the wall/**over** a ten-year period; **towards** the goal/**towards** success; **beyond** reason

- They can go with many verbs, adjectives and nouns:
  believe **in**/different **from**/characteristics **of**

- They can form part of a common phrase:
  to what extent/**in** contrast **to**/**in** line **with**/**on** account **of**

- They can form part of a phrasal verb:
  carry **out**/draw **on**/weigh **up**/account **for**
  ◗ See **54** *Using phrasal verbs.*

▶ Here are some examples of when you might need to use prepositions in academic work:

To report information (verbs)

White (2008) points **out**, admits **to**, agrees **to**/agrees **with** X **on/about** something, reflects **on**, accuses X **of**, refers **to**, expresses doubts/concerns **about/over**, draws attention **to**, focuses **on**, gives/lends support **to**

To introduce or describe research/a study, etc.

conduct research **into**, be involved **in**, do a study **on**, be based **on**, focus/centre **on**, the aim/focus **of**, find **out about**, an analysis **of**, provide evidence **of/for**, present findings/a paper **on**/an overview **of**

To describe and compare data/results, etc.

rise/increase **to**, align **with**, a rise/increase/difference **of/in**, correspond **to**, stabilise **at**, equivalent **to**, fluctuate **between**, be consistent **with**, peak **at**/(a) peak **of**, correlation **between**, a proportion **of**

To discuss advantages and disadvantages

an advantage/disadvantage/**of/of** '-ing', an advantage/disadvantage/benefit/drawback **for** someone, benefit **from**, be of benefit **to**

To define

define/name **as**, unique **to**, a description **of**, refer **to** X **as**, specific **to**, place an/the emphasis **on**, classify **into** (groups), inherent **in**, knowledge **about/of**, distinguish **between**, a definition **of**, an image/picture **of**

To describe cause and effect relationships

result **in**, dependent **on**, a repercussion **of**, a consequence/outcome **of**, implications **of**, an impact/effect/influence **on/of** X, a factor **in**

To give reasons and explanations

account **for**, an indication **of**, an example **of**, contribute **to**, point **to/towards**, a reason/justification

▶ Here are some additional points about prepositions and verbs:

- If a verb follows a preposition, the verb must be in the '-ing' form:
  Despite evidence to the contrary, Mackie (2017) insisted **on arguing** that he was right. ✔
  Despite evidence to the contrary, Mackie (2017) insisted **on argue** that he was right. ✖

- In formal English, it is often better to put the preposition before a relative pronoun:
  This is the research **on which** Cairns based her theory of molecular attraction. (*More formal.*) ✔
  This is the research that Cairns based her theory of molecular attraction **on**. (*Less formal.*) ✖

! **Danger Zone**

Omitting 'the fact (that)'

Sometimes you need to use 'the fact that':

The discussion focused on **the fact that** the results looked misleading. ✔

The discussion focused **on that** the results looked misleading. ✖

Exercises

1 Complete each gap with the correct preposition.

a The reviewers expressed some doubts .... the authenticity of the material and, as a result, the writer was accused .... plagiarism.

b When the results of the survey were analysed, it was observed that there had been an increase .... five percent .... reading scores, which was consistent .... previous years.

c The field trip, conducted by a group of geologists, was designed to provide the department .... a better overview .... the surrounding area.

d Some problems, inherent .... the nature of research and its narrow focus .... particular subjects or sub-groups, cannot be readily avoided.

e In order to account .... the discrepancies in their data, the research team drew their critics' attention .... some of the experimental constraints.

2 Rewrite the sentences so that the preposition does not come at the end.

a This is the area that we have most knowledge about.

b Here are the results that I based my assessment on.

c The survey identified individuals that there is no current provision for.

d You need to look at the groups the insects have been classified into.

e Sometimes there are problems that we do not have explanations for.

f It turned out to be a situation that most people benefited from.

51 Using prepositions (2)

A **correct preposition** clarifies meaning; an **incorrect** or **unnecessary** one obscures it.

You must comply ~~to~~ **with** the confidentiality agreement.
We will explore ~~on~~ this topic in the next session.

 Writing Tip

To produce clear, accurate written work, it is essential to know which prepositions to use with certain words and phrases. If you are not sure, check in a dictionary that has example sentences.

▶ Here are some reasons why mistakes are made using prepositions.

1 Sometimes different prepositions can be used with the same word

Meals were **provided for** the participants during the study. (*for + somebody*)
The results **provided** the researchers **with** the information that they needed. (*with + something*)

2 Sometimes the word is not followed by a preposition at all

The article **highlighted** ~~on~~ the main ideas of Peterson.
You might make this type of mistake because:

● A synonym of the word goes with the preposition:
highlight ~~on~~ → focus **on**   enhance ~~on~~ → improve **on**   comprise ~~of~~ → consist **of**

● The meaning of the word (wrongly) suggests that the preposition is needed:
eliminate ~~out~~ → 'out' carries the idea of something being removed

● A related phrase goes with the preposition:
to research ~~on~~ → to do research **on**
to emphasise ~~on~~ → to place emphasis **on**
to discuss ~~about~~ → to have a discussion **about**

● The verb can be used with and without the preposition, depending on the context and meaning:
Peterson **found** ~~out~~ several anomalies in his data.
Peterson **found out** why his data was corrupt.

3 Sometimes an object comes between a verb and its preposition

We have **devoted** all our time **to** this question.

NOTE: The further the preposition is from the verb, the greater the possibility for error.
The noise **distracted** everyone in the lecture hall ~~on~~ **from** the task.

Prepositional phrases

Phrases that start with prepositions can cause problems for students. Here are some examples of correct use:

In someone's view/from someone's point of view/in the view of

These are all ways of expressing people's opinions:
In Lyle's **view**/**From** Lyle's **point of view**, there is little support for such a theory.
In the view of some technicians, safety in the laboratory could be improved.

In view of/with a view to

The first phrase means 'because of'; the second means 'with the aim of'.
In view of the safety issues, the laboratory has been temporarily closed.
Work is being undertaken, **with a view to** re-opening the laboratory in the next few days.

With the exception of/except for

Both phrases mean 'apart from'; the first is more formal.
All the experiments took place on the campus **with the exception of/except for** the control test.

In line with/in keeping with

These phrases mean 'consistent with' or 'in the same style as'.
The arguments put forward by Browne are **in line with** current thinking.
It is important for the tone of a piece of writing to be **in keeping with** its general purpose.

 Remember!

Some common phrases are widely misused:
There is no point ~~of~~ **in** doing research on a very small sample.
All the statistics supported the theory except ~~from~~ **for** the final batch.

With regard to/in terms of

The first phrase means 'in connection with'; the second clarifies the particular issue you wish to discuss.
A great deal of discussion took place **with regard to** the outcome of the trial.
The trial was well run **in terms of** its timing but other aspects could have been better organised.

In respect of/with respect to/in connection with

Both phrases mean 'on the subject of' or 'regarding'.
I am writing **in respect of/with respect to/in connection with** my recent application.

On account of/in the light of

Both phrases introduce a reason or an explanation.
No work will be done on the project **on account of** the staff shortage.
In the light of increasing student numbers, more research staff have been taken on.

On reflection/in retrospect/with hindsight

The first phrase means 'thinking about it'; the second and third mean 'looking back'.
On reflection, it would have been better to use a different method of analysis.
The emphasis placed on external influences was, **in retrospect/in hindsight**, too great.

Exercises

1 Choose the correct alternative to complete the sentences.

a The researchers *found/found out* some anomalies in their data.
b Some people have devoted their lives *to/in* the pursuit of knowledge.
c Everyone *except from/apart from* Goh has supported this theory.
d I have decided to *research/research on* a different area.
e The equipment *comprises of/consists of* a bell jar, a funnel and a tube.
f There is no point *of/in* presenting a claim if you cannot back it up.

2 Complete the gaps in the sentences with the correct noun.

a No differences were found with .... to drug tolerance levels.
b All layout and design features must be in .... with standard practice.
c In Graham's ...., more research is needed before any definitive conclusions can be drawn.
d On .... of the huge turnout, the lecture room was changed at the last minute.
e In ...., better results might have been achieved had the final phase been less rushed.
f Nothing has been agreed in .... of future research plans.
g All analyses in this investigation, with the .... of one, were completed on time.
h Certain activities have been cut from the budget in the .... of the economic downturn.

52 Creating longer words

At its worst, according to Stern (2019), business forecasting is a science that cannot be relied upon, hiding itself in language that we cannot comprehend.	→	At its worst, according to Stern (2019), business forecasting is an **unreliable** science, hiding itself in **incomprehensible** language.

 Writing Tip

Using longer, more complex words in an appropriate way will improve the quality and style of your work.

Forming longer words

This often involves adding a prefix and/or suffix to a word to create a longer and more complex word:

think → unthinkable   appear → disappearance   theory → theoretically

Prefixes, such as *in-*, *ir-*, *dis-*, *un-* and *non-*, are added to the beginning of words. They often give words a negative or an opposite meaning; e.g. *relevant* → *irrelevant*.

NOTE: Some prefixes, such as *non-*, are followed by a hyphen → *non-existent*.

Suffixes, such as *-ly*, *-ful*, *-wise*, *-able* and *-ness*, are added to the ends of words to modify their meaning. They often change the part of speech: e.g. *enjoy* (verb) → *enjoyable* (adjective).

Using longer words

▶ **Read this paragraph from a business case study and look at the words used to express the key ideas.**

> When consultants were called in to advise on how the organisation should **implement** change, they **recommended** several things. They **advised against** rapid change and suggested that management should **consult** staff on the subject for a fairly **long** period. They said that some of the ideas the management were **proposing** would **not work** because they were too **complex,** and they mentioned how **unpopular** the suggested productivity scheme would be. The consultants also stressed the need for management and staff to work together in **harmony**.

● Here is the paragraph with longer word forms:

> When consultants were called in to advise the organisation on the **implementation** of change, they made several **recommendations**. They said that rapid change was **inadvisable** and suggested a **lengthy** period of **consultation** between management and staff. They described some of the management's **proposals** as **unworkable** because of their **complexity** and mentioned the likely **unpopularity** of the productivity scheme. They also stressed the need for management and staff to work together **harmoniously**.

Using suffixes and prefixes to enhance vocabulary use

Nouns:	**Indecisiveness** at senior management level and **misfortune** in terms of global market conditions proved to be a fatal **combination**.
Adjectives:	The **innovative** approach taken to marketing was the main **contributory** factor in the **extraordinary** success of the product.
Adverbs:	**Initially**, they felt that it would be best to proceed **cautiously**, and so they **temporarily** kept staffing at the lowest possible level.
Verbs:	Rather than **endanger** the whole future of the company, the board decided to **minimise** expenditure on speculative projects and to **strengthen** its core operations.

Danger Zone

Spelling mistakes

When you add a prefix and/or suffix to a word (affixation), existing letters may change:

e.g. *temporary* → *temporarily*   *temporaryly* ✗

Although there are some spelling rules for affixation, they are hard to remember and there are many exceptions – it is better to learn how to spell each individual word.

The comment was **un**necessary and **un**helpful. ✓

unecessary ✗
unhelpfull ✗

▶ See **59** *Key spelling rules* and **60** *Common spelling mistakes*.

Exercises

1 Create the correct longer words from the words in brackets.

a The .... (*likely*) of further .... (*certain*) in the travel sector .... (*strong*) the board's view that .... (*expand*) should be put on hold.

b Although the aviation industry is a major (*contribute*) .... to the (*environment*) .... problems we face today, the rise in air travel seems to be (*stop*) ....

c The company decided to carry out a critical (*assess*) .... of their business systems as many of them had become (*date*) .... and were causing certain sectors to (*perform*) ....

d In all (*probable*) ...., the (*technology*) .... innovations taking place will bring about a (*transform*) .... of the industry.

e His time as CEO of the company was (*character*) .... by a (*disappoint*) .... (*imagine*) .... approach to (*lead*) ....

2 Rewrite this paragraph, replacing the underlined words with longer words.

People <u>disagreed</u> as to which course of action would have the most <u>effect</u>. The company's founders felt with some <u>passion</u> that their position was the correct one and they had <u>no sympathy</u> with the views of others. This is an <u>example</u> of the kind of struggle that was going on within many organisations at the time.

3 Use a prefix to make these words mean the opposite or have a negative meaning.

a heartening ....   g respective ....

b logical ....   h orderly ....

c justifiable ....   i consistent ....

d estimate ....   j natural ....

e conceivable ....   k legal ....

f compliant ....   l pure ....

Writing Tip

Sometimes, the use of a single, complex word instead of a basic or common phrase can have an impact on the reader. It can help to make your writing more serious and academic in style. As you write, think carefully about the words you use. Make sure they are the most appropriate and that they express your ideas precisely.

Forming a longer word using a prefix or suffix

◆ (See **52** *Creating longer words*)

When the councillor read the minutes of the meeting, he found that his views had not been presented properly.

When the councillor read the minutes of the meeting, he found that his views had been **misrepresented**.

Using one word instead of a spoken phrase

Some members of the council had to make the same point <u>again and again</u> before it was addressed.

Some members of the council had to make the same point **repeatedly** before it was addressed.

Using a precise word instead of a phrase

<u>A list of items for discussion</u> at the next meeting was prepared.

An **agenda** for the next meeting was prepared.

▶ **Read this extract from an economics essay. Think about places where a phrase could be replaced by a single, powerful word.**

It soon became apparent that such a high level of growth could not be sustained. Questions then arose as to what should be put first. Politicians wanted to make sure that existing standards of living were safe but many economists had a different point of view. They felt that taking only a short-term view was a mistake, even if the desire to do this was easy to understand. What could not be disputed, however, was that the country was entering a new economic phase.

● Here is the extract with more precise wording:

It soon became apparent that such a high level of growth was **unsustainable**. Questions then arose as to what should be **prioritised**. Politicians wanted to **safeguard** existing standards of living but many economists thought **differently**. They felt that taking only a short-term view was a mistake, even if the **desirability** of doing this was **understandable**. What was **indisputable**, however, was that the country was entering a new economic phase.

 Danger Zone

Non-existent words

Make sure that you use a word that really exists! For example, if the word is a negative or opposite one, be sure that it begins with the correct prefix (*un-*, *in-* or *dis-*, etc.).

The research was ~~unconclusive~~ because some of the results were ~~contradictive~~. ✗
The research was **inconclusive** because some of the results were **contradictory**. ✓

- Here are some more examples:

The need for tough economic measures <u>could not be denied</u>.	→	The need for tough economic measures was **undeniable**.
When the tax rules were <u>made clearer</u>, revenues from taxation rose <u>a great deal</u>.	→	When the tax rules were **clarified**, revenues from taxation rose **considerably**.
<u>People who are against</u> the idea say that high taxation <u>causes people not to want to</u> work hard.	→	**Opponents** of the idea say that high taxation is a **disincentive** to hard work.
Some measures had effects that <u>were not foreseen</u> and caused the situation to <u>get worse</u>.	→	Some measures had **unforeseen** effects that caused the situation to **deteriorate**.

Exercises

1 Complete the rewritten sentences, using one word instead of the underlined phrase. Form the word from one of the underlined words.

a <u>There can be no doubt that</u> this is one of the most urgent problems facing many governments today.
..........., this is one of the most urgent problems facing many governments today.

b The new legislation was <u>impossible</u> for most people, even experts, <u>to comprehend</u>.
The new legislation was .... to most people, even experts.

c The Minister felt that the public had <u>understood</u> her words <u>in the wrong way</u>.
The Minister felt that the public had .... her words.

d The Foreign Office believes that if the UK can broker a peace settlement in the region, the local economic gains would be so great that they could <u>not be measured</u>.

2 Complete the rewritten sentences, using one word instead of the underlined phrase.

a The results of this management theory were <u>not the same in every case</u>.
The results of this management theory were *var...........* .

b This incident <u>showed clearly</u> a major problem within the organisation.
This incident *high...........* a major problem within the organisation.

c Unfortunately the country lacked the <u>basic services and systems needed by the company</u>.
Unfortunately the country lacked the necessary *infra...........* .

d A problem with cash flow often leads to <u>companies going out of business</u>.
A problem with cash flow often leads to *ban...........* .

e The pressure of <u>prices going up</u> can cause governments or central banks to increase interest rates.
Inf........... pressure can cause governments or central banks to increase interest rates.

54 Using phrasal verbs

A **phrasal verb** consists of a **verb** and an **adverb** or **preposition** or both:

'carry out' → Researchers **carried out** an experiment.

The meaning of a phrasal verb is often different from any usual meaning of the verb or any logical meaning of the phrase. This phrasal verb means 'perform' or 'conduct'. It does not describe physically carrying something and it does not describe something being 'out'.

 Writing Tip
Many phrasal verbs are used in informal, spoken language and are not appropriate for academic writing. Others, however, are appropriate and useful in academic writing. Make sure you know which ones to use.

Informal use of phrasal verbs

▶ **Read the following paragraph from a business essay, thinking about which words or phrases should be avoided in formal writing, and how you would replace them.**

> Some small companies get by for many years by putting off difficult decisions. If a business is to thrive, however, it needs to pick out its weaknesses and face up to the challenges of operating in the modern business environment. A recession, for example, may be an ideal time to check out successful competitors and come up with new business ideas. Going for that approach is better than hanging on in the hope that something turns up and tides the company over until better conditions return.

What's wrong: Some phrasal verbs (*get by, dip into, tide over, turn up*) are normally too informal for academic use.

- Many phrasal verbs have direct, more formal equivalents:

  get by → survive   put off → postpone   pick out → identify   face up to → confront
  check out → investigate   come up with → devise   go for → choose

- Others can be 'translated' into more formal English, sometimes by using another phrase. In the context above, you could write:

  hang on → take no action   turns up → appears by chance
  tides the company over → keeps the company solvent

▶ **Here is a rewritten version of the paragraph:**

> Some small companies **survive** for many years by **postponing** difficult decisions. If a business is to thrive, however, it needs to **identify** and **confront** the challenges of operating in the modern business environment. A recession, for example, may be an ideal time to **investigate** successful competitors and **devise** new business ideas. **Choosing** that approach is better than **taking no action** in the hope that something **appears by chance** and **keeps the company solvent** until better conditions return.

Phrasal verbs used in academic writing

allow for (include when planning)
In her study, Professor Cresswell **allows for** the fact that members of the public sometimes exaggerate their accounts.

bail out (rescue financially)
Most economists agree that the Government had no choice but to **bail out** a number of financial institutions in 2008.

bring about (cause to happen)
Discussions can sometimes **bring about** a satisfactory end to strike action.

call for something (make a public demand)
Three public sector unions have **called for** strike action if changes are not made to the programme of cuts.

call on/for someone *to ...* (demand action)
Human rights activists **called on/for** the Government **to** impose economic sanctions on the regime.

draw on (use resources)
Phillips **draws on** a considerable body of research to make his case.

hold up (remain strong)
Critics suggest that some of Britt's arguments do not **hold up** under scrutiny.

keep to (be relevant)
Stein has been accused of not **keeping to** the subject in his more controversial articles.

put forward (propose)
Gregory **puts forward** three key arguments in the first part of her report.

set out (present)
The case for change is clearly **set out** in the last of the team's publications.

set up (establish)
A panel of enquiry was **set up** to investigate the need for legislation in the area.

speak out about/against (speak publicly)
A number of protestors have **spoken out** about/against the treatment they received in prison.

take on (assume responsibility for)
A committee of MPs has **taken on** the task of overhauling outdated laws on computer hacking.

weigh up (consider carefully)
Peterson **weighs up** both options in his paper, before making a recommendation.

Exercises

1 Rewrite these sentences, replacing each underlined phrase with a more formal alternative.

a It may take a small business more than a year to <u>get over</u> a quarterly fall in sales.
b During the train strike, Edgo plc <u>laid on</u> a special bus service to take employees from the factory to the head office.
c A tier of middle managers were <u>laid off</u>, and six junior staff were appointed to replace them.
d In times of recession, companies often <u>cut back on</u> seasonal and temporary staff.
e Some consumers are likely to feel they are being <u>ripped off</u> if the monthly cost of calls rises dramatically.
f <u>Getting</u> your ideas <u>across</u> in a concise way is the key to success in a presentation.
g A meeting was called in an attempt to <u>sort out</u> the dispute.

2 Complete the gaps in these sentences with the most appropriate phrasal verb from the box. You may need to change the form of the verb.

weigh up	set up	hold up	speak out	call for	draw on

a Stevens argued that a committee should be .... to consider the new proposals.
b Some whistleblowers will .... even when their jobs are clearly at risk.
c After .... the pros and cons of the scheme, Polson suggested a realistic way forward.
d Barker .... her experience in Kenya to argue for an international summit on protecting tigers.
e Several prominent figures .... the Minister's resignation.
f Errors in their statistics meant that their argument did not ....

55 Collocations (1)

Words that are often seen or used together are called **collocations**.

You would write '*highly* **successful**', for example, rather than '*greatly* successful' or '*in-depth* **discussion**' rather than '*deep* discussion', even though all are grammatically correct.

 Writing Tip

Academic texts contain many examples of collocations that are common to this style of writing. Learning some of these and using them accurately will give a natural flow and an academic tone to your work.

▶ **Read this short paragraph on social mobility and look at the phrases in bold.**

Studies suggest that **social mobility** is reduced in societies where household incomes **vary significantly**. The greater the rewards from top jobs, the more likely it is that wealthier parents will seek to ensure that their children, in a **highly competitive** labour market, secure them. As the report by Hills (2018) **demonstrates clearly**, a **primary aim** of those with higher incomes is to make sure that their children, through education, also achieve this financial position. The link between house prices and proximity to good state schools, for example, is **widely accepted**.

Adjective + noun collocations

brief + account, description, discussion, history, introduction, overview, period, review, summary
final + analysis, answer, decision, outcome, phase, result, section, stage, step, version

In the **final section** of the report, Blake (2016) provides a **brief description** of new areas of research.

primary + aim, concern, focus, function, objective, purpose, reason, responsibility, source
significant + amount, contribution, factor, growth, impact, improvement, part, reduction
considerable + amount, debate, evidence, extent, influence, interest, research, support, variation

A **significant reduction** in town centre activity can lead to an increase in social isolation.
There has been **considerable interest** in the anti-pollution measures taken by local activists.

political + activism, agenda, arena, consensus, debate, (in)stability, movement, representation
social + attitudes, background, exclusion, identity, inequality, mobility, status, trend

Governments often insist that raising taxes does not form part of their **political agenda**.

NOTE: These nouns may be followed by a preposition, as in three of the examples above.
▶ See **50** and **51** *Using prepositions.*

 Remember!

There are thousands of common word partnerships in academic English. The ones you see in this unit and in unit 56 are a useful, small selection designed to draw your attention to the concept of collocation in a range of subject areas.

Adverb + adjective/past participle

highly + competitive, complex, controversial, critical, desirable, skilled, significant, successful
Marshall (2019) is **highly critical** of two of the investment schemes offered to pensioners.

increasingly + aware, common, complex, difficult, important, popular, sophisticated
Methods of avoiding tax have become **increasingly sophisticated** (Katz, 2020).

clearly + defined, demonstrated, established, identified, related
The link between rural poverty and higher levels of suicide is **clearly established** in the report.

widely + accepted, adopted, believed, discussed, known, recognized, regarded, shared, used
Schemes to increase the number of cycling paths have been **widely adopted** in Kent and Surrey.

NOTE: some adverbs regularly collocate with a particular past participle to produce a more specific meaning, e.g.: casually employed, newly appointed, privately financed, randomly chosen.

Verb + adverb

analyse + closely, systematically; **change** + constantly, dramatically, rapidly; **consider** + carefully, seriously; **demonstrate** + clearly, conclusively; **differ** + considerably, significantly, widely; **establish** + conclusively, firmly; **examine** + critically, thoroughly; **occur** + frequently, naturally; **study** + closely, thoroughly; **treat** + differently, equally; **use** + effectively, sparingly; **vary** + considerably, greatly, significantly, widely; **write** + authoritatively, convincingly, knowledgeably

Hall's recent research **establishes conclusively** that there is no written form of this dialect.
Sotra (2015) **writes authoritatively** on the patriarchal structure of these early communities.
Scientists have **systematically analysed** the evidence without finding a genetic link to the illness.

NOTE: As in the final example above, adverbs may sometimes precede verbs.

Exercises

1 Choose the most appropriate option in italics.

a Political *solidity/stability/reliability* is normally a requirement for a nation's wealth-creating plans.
b In terms of trade, China has considerable *emphasis/weight/influence* on the regime on North Korea.
c Doctors were unable to establish *firmly/tightly/strongly* a link between the injury and the blackouts.
d Small businesses have a significant *pressure/force/impact* on a country's economic prosperity.
e The primary *centre/target/focus* of Hayek's research in forensic linguistics is author identification.
f Regional development requires a workforce that is *deeply/highly/hugely* skilled.
g Attitudes towards food consumption vary *widely/broadly/generally* among countries.

2. Complete the adverbs in these sentences.

a Cycling is one of the *in............* popular options for urban commuters.
b The enquiry panel considered the evidence *ca............* over a period of ten weeks in 2020
c Conspiracy theories demonstrate *cl............* a desire to 'believe against the facts', notes Var (2017).
d Thomson's research examines *cr............* the policy's effect on poorer communities.
e The factors that led to the Vietnam war are studied *cl............* in Mann's article.
f Three of the projects developed by Southwark Council were *pr............* financed.
g Rules governing access to the government archive and the use of its material are *hi............* complex.

Writing Tip

Learning a wide range of natural collocations and being able to use them in an instinctive way gives you time to focus on other important aspects of your writing. Look at texts in your subject area and highlight collocations. Record the ones that you think will be useful to you. It may be helpful to give them a context by writing down some of the text that comes before and after them.

▶ Read this short paragraph on health care in low-income countries and note the language in bold.

A report by the World Health Organization (2019) **made** a **prediction** that, by 2030, there would be a short-fall in low-income countries of 18 million **health workers**, unless there was a significant change in **government policies**. The report **considered** the **evidence** from 28 such countries where **health services** were thought to be under serious pressure and, once again, **raised** the **issue** of the increasing migration of medical staff to higher-income countries.

Verb + noun collocations

carry out + an analysis of, an assessment of, an experiment, an investigation into, research, a task
consider + the evidence, the impact on, the implications of, an issue, the possibility of, the role of
give + consent, an explanation for, feedback, guidance, an overview of, a presentation on, priority to

The implications of the new law were **considered** in detail at the conference.
According to medical ethics, a patient must **give consent** before receiving treatment.

identify + an area, the cause of, factors, the features of, the issues, a problem, a way to (+ verb)
make + adjustments to, an argument, an assessment of, an assumption, a comment on, a contribution to, a distinction between, an impact on, an observation, a prediction, recommendations

Myers (2018) suggests that **identifying a way to** protect computers from this virus is impossible.
Roberts (2020) **makes a distinction** between bullying and harassment in the workplace.

provide + access to, assistance, benefits, care, evidence, an example of, an explanation for, feedback, guidance, information, input, an insight into, an opportunity for, an overview of, a service, support
raise + awareness of, funds for, an issue, morale, the possibility of, the price of, a question, standards

A solicitor will **provide guidance** in the drafting of a complex will.
A committee was then set up to **raise funds** for essential repairs to the mosque.

NOTE: The nouns listed above are preceded by 'a/an', 'the' or no article, and are in singular or plural form, according to common usage. This may change, however, depending on the context of your writing. Where a noun is often followed by a particular preposition, the preposition is given here.

Noun + noun collocations

Many nouns combine with other nouns to form partnerships such as 'climate change' or 'computer graphics'. Below are useful nouns with multiple partners.

business + community, empire, environment, objective, opportunity, sector, trip
Business communities may set up forums to discuss the closure of local retail outlets.

government + approval, cut, department, expenditure, grant, intervention, policy
Simons and Johnson (2017) discuss **government policy** on the regulation of news outlets.

health + care, centre, cut, hazard, insurance, problem, scare, service, worker
The source of this particular **health scare** was traced to three Facebook groups.

Information + desk, flow, gathering, processing, retrieval, sharing, source, system, technology
Developing an accurate algorithm is crucial in the process of **information retrieval**.

learning + curve, difficulties, experience, objective, outcome, process, resources, style
Teaching based on the idea of individual **learning styles** is problematic, according to Toms (2017).

research + centre, data, department, evidence, findings, grant, interests, methods, proposal
Research proposals must be approved by the department and may be awarded a grade.

Exercises

1 **Choose nouns from this list to complete the sentences:** awareness, role, assessment, benefits, contribution, causes, access

   a A good public transport system can make a positive .... to the local economy.
   b An .... of the financial impact of 'greener' policies was carried out at a local level.
   c Another storage option is to digitise everything, and give password .... to those who need it.
   d Regular physical exercise provides many .... to the health of the nation.
   e The purpose of the conference was to raise .... of the mental health pressures on care workers.
   f This report will begin by identifying several .... of underachievement in secondary schools.
   g Willis (2020) considers the .... of regional mayors and comments on their growing importance.

2 **Choose nouns from this list to complete the sentences:** gathering, workers, problems, outcome, grants, environment, cuts, findings

   a Oxford Solutions have maintained a solid performance in a very difficult business ....
   b The charity Mindset has been put at risk by the loss of two substantial government ....
   c Butler's data suggests that vegetarians are less prone to diet-related health ....
   d In her research ...., Berry links parental reading habits to the educational development of their children.
   e Information .... is the primary function of market research, according to Selcott (2019).
   f A good learning .... should make clear to students what they are expected to achieve by the end of the course.

Some words are often confused. This is usually because they have a similar form or sound, even though their meanings differ.

The Cultural revolution was a **historic** event in China.	→	being or taking place in the past and becoming significant in history
The book provides a **historical** account of the events leading up to the Cultural Revolution.	→	based on an analysis of important events in history

 Writing Tip

Your spellchecker will not pick up errors with these words because the mistakes involve words that do exist but are being used wrongly. Learn the meaning and spelling of these words, incorporate them into your writing and make sure you use them correctly.

▶ Here are some examples of words that are commonly confused.

1   Words that are in the same general area of meaning

advice	The noun (a piece of advice)
advise	The verb (consultants who advise the Government)
	My ~~advise~~ **advice** is that you should learn when to use 'c' and when to use 's'.
affect	The verb (which will affect many people)
effect	The noun (which will have an effect on many people)
	Changes in policy had a major ~~affect~~ **effect** on immigration numbers.

2   Words that have a different meaning

adverse	An adjective meaning *negative, not good* or *unhelpful* (adverse weather conditions)
averse	An adjective used with **to**, meaning *not liking* or *opposed to*
	Older people are sometimes ~~adverse~~ **averse to** change.
allusion	A noun meaning *an indirect reference to something*
illusion	A noun meaning *a false idea or belief*
	Patients were **under the** ~~allusion~~ **illusion that** the drug was making them better.
apprise	Used in the pattern apprise someone of something, meaning *inform*
appraise	Used with a noun, meaning *assess* or *evaluate* (appraise an employee)
	The President was ~~appraised~~ **apprised of** the latest developments in the crisis.
censor	A verb or noun related to *censorship*
sensor	A noun used to describe a *device that senses change or presence*
	The robot is fitted with ~~censors~~ **sensors** that can detect any obstacle in its path.
complementary	Used to describe *features or characteristics that go together well*
complimentary	Used to describe *praising someone or something*
	Leadership and public speaking are ~~complimentary~~ **complementary** skills.
economic	An adjective meaning *relating to the economy* (an economic downturn)
economical	An adjective meaning *saving or not wasting money*
	In a time of recession, many people are forced to adopt a more ~~economic~~ **economical** lifestyle.
insure	A verb linked to *insurance*
ensure	A verb meaning *make sure*
assure	A verb meaning *to remove any doubts someone may have about something*
	We need to ~~insure~~ ~~assure~~ **ensure** that these materials are handled with care.

elicit	A verb meaning *to draw a reaction or an opinion from someone*
illicit	An adjective used to refer to something that is *illegal*
	The company's ~~elicit~~ **illicit** practices brought it to the attention of the authorities.
eminent	An adjective that means *respected in a field of study*
imminent	An adjective that means *about to happen*
	Professor Jonathan White is an ~~imminent~~ **eminent** researcher in the field of biochemistry.
emigrate	A verb used to refer to *people leaving a country to go to another one*
immigrate	A verb used to refer to *people entering a country from another one*
	In the 1950s and 1960s many UK citizens ~~immigrated~~ **emigrated** to Australia.
imply	A verb used to *suggest something without saying it*
infer	A verb used to *deduce something that has not been directly stated*
	In his report, Dr Star ~~infers~~ **implies** that some of the council's recommendations are naive.
incidence	A noun meaning *the frequency with which something happens*
incident	A noun meaning *an event or something that happens*
	During the recession, there was a higher ~~incidents~~ **incidence** of mental health problems among the population.
loose	An adjective meaning *the opposite of tight*
lose	A verb meaning *the opposite of find or gain*
	During this period, Britain began to ~~loose~~ **lose** its influence in world affairs.
refute	A verb meaning *to prove that a theory, opinion, idea, etc. is wrong*
reject	A verb meaning *to be unwilling to accept something*
	Simonds ~~refutes~~ **rejects** the notion that Dickens influenced our understanding of the social issues of his period.

Exercises

1 Choose the correct alternative in italics.

a Net immigration figures take into account the number of *immigrants/emigrants* as well as the number of people coming into a country.

b Once the peace talks had broken down, everyone realised that war was *eminent/imminent*.

c The organising body *assured/ensured/insured* participants that no one would have an unfair advantage.

d If he persists with the road-building scheme, the councillor will *lose/loose* his seat.

e The author does not refer to herself; nevertheless, readers can *infer/imply* an autobiographical element.

f The *economic/economical* history of the country from 1950 to 1975 is covered in the article.

g Some very *complementary/complimentary* remarks were made during the prize-giving ceremony.

h British Sign Language *is composed/comprises* of different signs from its American counterpart.

2 Use a word from this unit to fill each of the gaps in this paragraph.

The installation of a piece of modern art has to be undertaken in consultation with those who live in the city and who will see it every day. Failure to do this has sometimes resulted in an unpleasant (a) .... Of primary importance is the need to (b) .... the views of citizens prior to the installation. This will (c) .... that no one can say, at the end of the process, that he or she was not consulted. If the local council takes expert (d) .... and canvasses as many opinions as possible, it will find that this also has a positive (e) .... on relationships. People who are (f) .... to the idea will be able to make their feelings clear and those responsible will be (g) .... of the general reaction and act accordingly. The unveiling of a major work of art in a city should be a (h) .... occasion enjoyed by all, rather than something that is seen as an unwelcome event.

Homonyms are words that sound the same but are spelt differently. They may be different parts of speech and may have different meanings.

As an author, she ~~new~~ **knew** exactly how much research she needed to do for her next novel.

 Writing Tip

Homonyms are often simple, basic words. Their confusion can result in serious errors, which may not be recognised by your editing tools. They may occur because you are writing too quickly or because of carelessness, so it is important to check your work before you hand it in.

▶ Here are some examples of homonyms that are commonly confused.

aloud/allowed

No collaboration was ~~aloud~~ **allowed** between the parties during the course of the investigation.

bare/bear

The freezing temperatures made living on the ~~bear~~ **bare** essentials even more challenging than usual. (= basic)
Councils had to ~~bare~~ **bear** the full costs of the scheme. (= supply/accept)
Local residents could not ~~bare~~ **bear** further noise from the airport. (= tolerate)

born/borne

These doubts were ~~born~~ **borne out** by later events. (= proved correct)

break/brake

At one point, there was serious concern that talks between the parties would ~~brake~~ **break** down but, fortunately, this did not happen.

counsel/council

The need to ~~council~~ **counsel** war veterans is much more widely accepted than it used to be. (= advise and support)
The ~~counsel~~ **council** failed to allocate sufficient funds to the project.

here/hear

More longitudinal studies are required on the impact of electronic noise on people's ability to ~~here~~ **hear**.

licence (noun)/license (verb)

A ~~license~~ **licence** is required for premises to have live music performances.
NOTE: In American English both the noun and verb are **license** with an 's'.

past/passed

Only three years have ~~past~~ **passed** since the disaster occurred.

practice (noun)/practise (verb)

This is common ~~practise~~ **practice** in the industry.
To ~~practice~~ **practise** medicine in this country, you will need to pass a language test.
NOTE: In American English both the noun and verb are **practice** with a 'c'.

principle/principal

Conservation is one of the ~~principle~~ **principal** concerns of biologists today. (= main)
He refused, on the grounds that it was against his ~~principals~~ **principles**. (= beliefs)
Mrs Johnson has just been made principal of the college. (= head of educational institution)

site/sight

People demonstrated against the proposal to use the area as the ~~sight~~ **site** for a nuclear reactor.

weather/whether

Several criteria must be taken into account when deciding ~~weather~~ **whether** or not to upgrade an existing building. NOTE: The word 'wether' does not exist.

Remember!

Use **too** (not 'to') with the meanings 'more than is wanted' and 'also':
The cost was ~~to~~ **too high**.
The plan was complex and it was very expensive ~~to~~ **too**.

 Danger Zone

its/it's

its is a possessive	They discussed the organisation of the project and **its** costs.
it's = 'it is'	**It's** a difficult problem to solve.

there/their/they're

there is the subject of a verb	and **there** were several unforeseen consequences
there is also an adverb	but the argument does not end **there**
their is a possessive	older people and **their** needs
they're = they are	and **they're** all serious issues

your/you're

your is a possessive	fill in **your** details below
you're = you are	**you're** making a mistake

who's/whose

who's = who is/who has	the person **who's** in charge of the office
whose is a possessive	someone **whose** judgement I trust

Exercises

1 Six of these sentences contain a mistake. Find the mistakes and correct them.

a Unlike many laws of physics, Archimedes' Principal is over two thousand years old.

b Actions that had been agreed at the strategy meeting turned out to be to costly to implement.

c A clear distinction has to be made between pushing the boundaries and actually breaking them.

d The biodiversity reserve has aloud previously threatened plant species to survive.

e Problems such as dyslexia often past unnoticed in the 1960s.

f Candidates were advised to submit applications as quickly as possible to be sure of a place.

g Not knowing weather to save money or invest it is a common problem these days.

h Perfectionists often cannot bare to be criticised.

2 Correct the ten mistakes in this paragraph.

One of the problems that arises when your paying for something over the internet is that you never see whose receiving your details at the other end. We like to think that their trustworthy but its impossible to know wether that is the case. As anyone whose been the victim of credit-card fraud will know, it can be very difficult to regain you're faith in online shopping once your identity has been stolen. Shops and restaurants may seem safer, but just as much fraud goes on their as it does on the web. These days, customers need reassurance that their transactions are safe and banks need to raise there game with regard to financial security. For all it's advantages, the online world can certainly have its downside.

Words are made up of **vowels** (a, e, i, o, u) and **consonants** (b, c, d, etc.).
Some words, such as phenomenon, are hard to spell and there are often no rules to help you.
Other words have **prefixes** and/or **suffixes** (e.g. insensitivity) and their spelling may adhere to certain rules.

 Writing Tip

Although English spelling can be difficult, try to remember some of the rules that are given in this section as they will help you correct or avoid mistakes. However, bear in mind that the rules sometimes have exceptions.

Words ending in 'e'

Drop the final 'e'

if the suffix begins with a vowel or if '-ing' is added

refuse → refus**al**   write → writ**ing**

Exceptions include some '-able' adjectives, such as knowledgeable, likeable.
This rule does not apply to words ending '-ee', e.g. guaranteeing, freeing.

Keep the final 'e'

if the suffix begins with a consonant or if '-d' is added

objective → objective**ly**   define → define**d**

Exceptions include truly and argument.

Words ending in 'y'

Change the final 'y' to 'ie'

if '-ed' is added to a verb that ends in a consonant + '-y'

comply → complied   verify → verified

Keep the 'y' if you are adding 'ing' (complying, verifying).

if '-er' or '-est' are added to an adjective

meaty → meatier   lively → liveliest

if 's' is added to a noun to make it plural

opportunity → opportunities   theory → theories

To form an adverb, change 'y' to 'ily'

funny → funnily   temporary → temporarily

Do not change the final 'y'

if 'ed' or 'ing' are added to a verb that ends in a vowel + 'y'

portray → portrayed   convey → conveying

Words ending in a consonant

Double the final consonant

if the word ends in one vowel + consonant

plan → planned   slip → slippery   plot → plotting

Exceptions include words ending in 'c' (which often becomes 'ck': panicking) and words ending in 'w' (growing), 'x' (fixed) or 'y' (stayed).

If the word ends with two vowels and a consonant, as in great → greatest, the letter is not usually doubled.

if the word ends in vowel + 'l'

virtual   →   virtually   logical   →   logically

Exceptions include fulfil → fulfilment.

Note also these words ending 'er':

prefer   →   preferring   →   preference
refer   →   referring   →   reference

and words ending 'it':

commit   →   committed   →   commitment   →   committee
elicit   →   elicited   →   eliciting
exhibit   →   exhibited   →   exhibiting

▶ See **10** *Using adverbs* and **52** *Creating longer words*.

Adding a prefix

- Adding a prefix does not usually change the spelling of a word, although it may necessitate the addition of a hyphen (non-).

- If the last letter of the prefix is the same as the first letter of a word, the new word you form will have a double letter:

misrepresented *but* misspelled   uneducated *but* unnecessary

NOTE: 'il' and 'ir' are only added to words that begin with 'l' and 'r', so the letter is always doubled: illogical, illiterate, irrelevant, irrefutable

Exercises

1 Correct the spelling of these words using the rules in this unit.

   a controling   e delightfull
   b diarys   f iregular
   c missquoted   g bidable
   d hygieneic   h dissapointed

2 Change the words in brackets into the correct form by adding a prefix, suffix or verb ending.

   a ………… (*open*) to change can signal a significant ………… (*improve*) in people diagnosed with Obsessive Compulsive Disorder.
   b The institution is ………… (*primary*) concerned with rehabilitation following a ………… (*stress*) illness.
   c Greater levels of ………… (*co-operate*) between staff and local governing bodies have led to ………… (*notice*) improvements in care.
   d The controversy arose because ministers' ………… (*argue*) had been ………… (*construed*).
   e The ………… (*set*) up of a respite care system marked an important ………… (*achieve*) for all concerned.
   f The study reflected on the ………… (*continuity*) of care and their effect on youngsters ………… (*await*) adoption.
   g Strategies used to encourage the prescription of drugs developed by selected pharmaceutical ………… (*company*) should be ………… (*prohibit*).
   h Researchers are aware that the social ………… (*behave*) of some patients with mental-health problems is not overly ………… (*similar*) to that of healthy people.

60 Common spelling mistakes

 Writing Tip

Spelling mistakes can ruin an otherwise excellent piece of academic work and can give a bad impression on a CV. Get into the habit of using a dictionary to make sure that you are spelling words correctly.

▶ **Read this paragraph from an essay on English literature and think about why the underlined words have been spelt wrongly. Then look at the reasons below.**

Jane Austen's novel *Pride and Prejudice* was, it seems, <u>quiet</u> carefully constructed. It makes a clear statement about moral values at the time she was <u>writting</u>, yet also has a timeless significance. Unlike some of her <u>contempories</u>, she restricted herself to the type of world she knew she was capable of reproducing in prose. She understood her own social <u>enviroment</u> and never went beyond this. As a result, the story presents a snapshot of 18th-century life, without <u>exagerration</u> or extremes. She <u>insured</u> that any detail was kept to a <u>mininum</u>. A close examination of the descriptive passages reveals little in the way of figurative language; few similes or metaphors; no <u>extraenous</u> emotion. The reader can be secure in the knowledge that there will be no distractions from the all-important plot.

1 Some words have silent letters or letters that are not clearly pronounced

She understood her own social ~~enviroment~~ **environment** and never went beyond this.

● Here are some more examples:

~~goverment~~	government	~~religous~~	religious
~~exibit~~	exhibit	~~densly~~	densely
~~psycology~~	psychology	~~assinement~~	assignment
~~neigbour~~	neighbour	~~garantee~~	guarantee

2 Some words are not spelt the way they sound

Unlike some of her ~~contempories~~ **contemporaries**, she restricted herself to the type of world she knew she was capable of reproducing in prose.

● Here are some more examples:

~~dependant~~	dependent	~~tempory~~	temporary
~~summery~~	summary	~~responsability~~	responsibility
~~definately~~	definitely	~~persue~~	pursue
~~seperate~~	separate	~~ditract~~	detract

3 Some words have a challenging mix of single and double letters

As a result, the story presents a snapshot of 18th-century life, without ~~exagerration~~ **exaggeration** or extremes.

● Here are some more examples:

~~acomodation~~	accommodation	~~appartment~~	apartment
~~inovation~~	innovation	~~asessment~~	assessment
~~abreviate~~	abbreviate	~~ocasion~~	occasion
~~fullfillment~~	fulfilment	~~embarass~~	embarrass
~~reccomend~~	recommend	~~necesary~~	necessary

4 Some words have vowel or consonant groups that pose problems

A close examination of the descriptive passages reveals little in the way of figurative language; few similes or metaphors; no ~~extraenous~~ **extraneous** emotion.

- Here are some more examples:

~~reciept~~	receipt	~~rythm~~	rhythm
~~hygeine~~	hygiene	~~pharoah~~	pharaoh
~~diareah~~	diarrhoea	~~langauge~~	language
~~twelth~~	twelfth	~~syncronise~~	synchronise

Remember!

The rhyme *'i' before 'e' except after 'c'* holds true for most words: receive, perceive, believe, reprieve, conceive. Exceptions include weird, weigh and neighbour.

5 Some words are commonly confused or misused

Jane Austen's novel *Pride and Prejudice* was, it seems, ~~quiet~~ **quite** carefully constructed. She ~~insured~~ **ensured** that any detail was kept to a mininum.

❧ See **57** *Commonly misused words* and **58** *Commonly confused words – homonyms.*

6 Some words have unexpected spelling changes when their form changes

It makes a clear statement about moral values at the time she was ~~writting~~ **writing**, yet also has a timeless significance.

❧ See **52** *Creating longer words.*

American versus British spelling

- Many institutions accept American or British spelling but whichever you use, it is important to be consistent. Common examples of differences include:

American	color	center	connexion	fulfill	catalog	kilometer
British	colour	centre	connection	fulfil	catalogue	kilometre

- Some words ending in 'ise', e.g. organise, criticise, publicise, are spelt with a 'z' in American English: organize, criticize, publicize. Many others, however, are not (televise).

Exercises

1 Decide which of these words is misspelt and write the correct spelling in the space provided.

a wierd ....
b necesary ....
c comittment ....
d integrated ....
e stabalise ....
f oppotunities ....
g excellence ....
h access ....
i successfull ....
j concieve ....

2 Each line in the paragraph contains one spelling mistake: underline it and write the correction in the space provided.

Graham Greene was an acomplished novelist of the 1930s. Although   ....
many of his books have a religous significance, he also caught the   ....
mood of his day, unlike many of his contempories who only gave a   ....
very faint idea of the harsh realaties of life in the shadows of war.   ....
Greene's knowlede and understanding of his society were drawn   ....
primerily from newspapers and, in this way, he was able to produce   ....
realistic caracters, rather than relying on fictional creations. Today   ....
he remains a much-loved writer whose tendency to potray life   ....
in somewhat pesimistic terms does not detract in any way from   ....
his overall appeal.

Like any other form of communication, an **email** should be written with the reader in mind.

 Writing Tip

An email will create a positive or negative impression on your tutor, depending on how it is written. However well you get on with your tutor, your correspondence should reflect your relative status, should be clear and easy to read, and should not contain mistakes.

Write a clear and useful subject line

Your tutor is a busy person and has an inbox full of emails. He or she needs to be able to note the content of a message quickly and to make any necessary response.

Subject: Hi!	**Subject:** Need a favour, please!	**Subject:** Quick question

What's wrong: At a glance, none of the subject lines gives any indication of what the email is about.

- Here is an example of a full, clear subject line:

Subject: Request work reference for Dave Watts, History 2006

 Remember!

Your email address may bear no relation to your name, so putting your name in the subject line may be helpful if your tutor has a lot of students. It may be useful to add your course details as well.

- Here are some further guidelines. Corrected versions for each can be found in the key on page 146.

Use correct grammar

Contractions (e.g. won't) are acceptable, but grammatical mistakes, even in a short message, can cause confusion and annoy the reader.

▶ **Find six grammatical errors in this email and add an appropriate subject line.**

Subject: ....

I'm really sorry but I'll be late handing in my assignment on care of the elderly. The due date's 27th of this month and I know I should of finished by then but I wonder if I hand it in a week later. I've been off sick with a really bad throat infection and didn't have time to do all the reading yet. I'd like to ask for a week's extension, would give me time to catch up. I hope my term grades isn't affected by this.

Tony Hill

Punctuate your email

A well-punctuated email is much easier to read than a poorly punctuated one.

▶ **Insert six punctuation marks in this email and make two additional changes.**

Ive just started the module on world Archaeology (3033) and am finding the topic a bit too broad. I realise that although I like the global coverage I would be better suited to something more specific as I've always had an interest in African Archaeology could I change to this module.

Make clear connections within sentences

Unnecessary repetition and inaccurate referencing should be avoided.

▶ **Replace the underlined words so that the connections are improved, and write an appropriate subject line.**

> Subject: ....
>
> I've decided to take part in the Mongol Rally next year, <u>it</u> involves driving a car from Europe to Mongolia over the summer vacation. I wonder if you'd be willing to sponsor me for <u>the Mongol Rally</u>. It's not a race and I'm not trying to win anything – <u>that's</u> all about making it to the end of the route and donating your vehicle to a local charity. I've always admired <u>them</u> people who take on a charitable cause, so I've decided to have a go at <u>these</u> myself. May I count on your support?

Make sure your sentences can be understood

You must ensure that everything you write makes clear sense.

▶ **Rewrite this email so that the sentences are correct and complete.**

> I'd like to change the topic for my presentation. I did say that I would do it on communication issues. Have previously worked on this. But I've found it very hard to find enough material or getting the right ideas. Now I think I have a better idea that I've been working on if it's okay if I do it on sensory deprivation instead?

Make sure style and function are appropriate

Although emails are informal, you should avoid using slang or poor expression when writing to your tutor.

▶ **Underline four words or phrases in this email that you think should be replaced.**

> **Subject:** Re our appointment
>
> I've just realised that I should have been meeting with you this morning! I dunno why I forgot but I feel really bad about it. I'd like to re-schedule the meeting if possible cos I still have some problems with my presentation. What about Friday at 10?

 Remember!

Read your email through before you send it. Like any other piece of writing, you won't get it right first time.

Use appropriate words and correct spelling

Like grammar mistakes, errors in vocabulary create a bad impression.

▶ **Find eight mistakes in word choice or spelling in this email.**

> I've just applied for a job as a volunteer in a charity shop and I need to provide the names of two people who know me but who aren't relatives. I'd really apreciate it if I could put you're name down as a reference. I think they'll contact you and it only involvs writing a short paragraph about me, outlining my skills and giving some information about my caracter. I don't think there's any point of writing a lot as it's only a tempory job.
>
> Could I also contact you for advise if I get an interview?

62 Covering letters and CVs

A **covering letter** states what position you are applying for, why you are interested in this type of work, how your skills match the job requirements and when you are available for interview.

A **CV** (curriculum vitae) describes your education, qualifications, work experience and skills, and is normally tailored to the post for which you are applying. In most CVs, subheadings on work experience and skills are followed by short explanatory texts.

 Writing Tip

The first impression you make on a prospective employer is likely to be through the quality of your writing in the covering letter and the CV that you send. Both items should be as brief and relevant as possible. They must also be grammatically accurate and written in an appropriate style.

Typical mistakes in covering letters and CVs

- misused words, which your spellchecker won't pick up
  I was able to ~~insure~~ **ensure** that ~~their~~ **there** were no further faults in the accounting system.
  ◗ See **57** *Commonly misused words* and **58** *Commonly confused words – homonyms*.

- punctuation errors
  My case study examined ineffective staff appraisal and ~~it's~~ **its** consequences.
  ◗ Pay particular attention to **20** *Commas 2: incorrect uses* and **23** *Apostrophes*.

- grammar errors
  Although the number of accidents at work ~~have~~ **has** fallen, the role of health and safety …
  ◗ See, in particular, **3** *Singular or plural subjects and verbs* and **35** *Incomplete sentences*.

 Danger Zone
Overusing and misusing capital letters

It is very important to use capital letters where they are needed – for actual courses, modules, institutions and job titles – but don't use them for making general references.

Having graduated with a BSc in finance from the university of Hull, I am keen to apply the Specialist Knowledge I have acquired in Accountancy and Statistics. ✖

> Having graduated with a BSc in finance from the University of Hull, I am keen to apply the specialist knowledge I have acquired in accountancy and statistics. ✔
> ◗ See **25** *Capital letters*.

Key grammar for covering letters

- Linking ◗ See **27** *Linking: adding* and **29** *Linking: results*.
  As well as/In addition to teaching me to work to tight deadlines, my role on the student newspaper required me to seek advertising revenue from local businesses.

- Participles ◗ See **34** *Participles*.
  I have extensive experience in the retail sector, **giving** me the skills to deal with all types of customers.

- Relative clauses ◗ See **15** *Relative clauses*.
  I am familiar with most of the techniques **that** are used in testing clinical samples.

- Emphasising ◗ See **11** *Emphasising*.
  What I learnt from leading the team **was** the importance of setting agreed goals.

Key grammar for CVs

- Gerunds ◗ See **13** *Gerunds and infinitives*.

June–Sept. 2020	**Box Office Assistant, Theatre Royal, Ilfracombe** This role **involved taking** phone calls, **accepting** payment and … In this role, I was **responsible for taking** phone calls, … **Dealing** with customer enquiries was the key aspect of this role …

- Giving examples ◗ See **42** *Introducing an example*.

I respond well to challenges and am flexible in seeking solutions.
An example of this is the way in which I designed a new system for promoting events.
This can be illustrated/exemplified by the new system I designed …

- Present perfect and past simple ◗ See **4** *Correct tense formation*.

I **joined** our debating society at school and **have continued** to take an interest in public speaking and presentations. In 2020 my university team **won** the Whitman Debating Cup.

 Remember!

It is acceptable to use abbreviated language in CVs, particularly in short sections involving lists.

Additional skills and posts held

- Fluent in German   (rather than 'I am fluent … ')
- Full current driving licence   (rather than 'I hold a full … ')
- Elected treasurer of the Choral Society   (rather than 'I was elected treasurer … ')

Exercises

1 Find and correct the mistakes in these extracts from covering letters.

a I am keen to gain experience in the world of Publishing, this is why I am writing to you.
b Having worked as a receptionist in a busy GP practise I believe I would respond well to the pressures of the post.
c My CV which you will find enclosed lists the various positions that I have held from 2017 to 2020, while I was a member of the student counsel.
d In the passed three years at college, not only I have taken evening classes in Chinese, but I have also made two trips to Beijing to visit Computer Trade Fairs.

2 Find and correct the mistakes in these extracts from CVs.

a To handle customer complaints was the most important part of this part-time post.
b 2018–2020   Rumworth Sixth Form college Leicester

             A-Levels; Biology (B), Physics (A, Maths (A*) French (C).

c Working as part of professor Robertson's research group helped me to develop complimentary skills in communication and teamwork. Which proved useful when I organised a presentation on our findings.
d Having a good knowledge of recent trends in online shopping are vital, in my view, to the Retail Industry which is why my final year dissertation focused on peoples' reasons for switching from popular high street outlets to internet retail sites.

Key

1 Parts of speech

Exercise 1

Nouns: course, qualification, graduates, positions, variety, professions, details, website, service, students, answers, queries
Verbs: provides, find, are, operate, can, get
Adjectives: useful, Full, available, advisory, prospective, clear
Adverbs: regularly, quickly
Prepositions: in, of, on, to
Pronouns: our, we, their
Articles: The, a, a, an
Linking words/phrases: and, Furthermore, so that

Exercise 2

a	4	e	2
b	2	f	6
c	5	g	1
d	3		

2 Parts of a sentence

Exercise 1

a Subject: pupils; main verb: can take; object: the International Baccalaureate
b Subject: many people; main verb: welcomed; object: comprehensive schools
c Subject: private schools; main verb: offer; object: scholarships

Exercise 2

a <u>Students applying for university places have to complete the application process</u>, which includes a personal statement.
b <u>The three categories of state schools during the 1960s were grammar, comprehensive and secondary modern.</u>
c In the 1990s, when polytechnics changed their name and became universities, <u>the overall number of applications for higher education places rose sharply</u>.

Exercise 3

a Three clauses:
   main clause: The system for the funding of higher education is a major issue in the UK
   dependent clauses: which has changed several times over the past few decades; affecting a great many families

b Three clauses:
   main clause: British universities have long attracted overseas students
   dependent clauses: because of their high reputation; these students have become an important source of revenue
c Two clauses:
   main clause: the variety of courses on offer at British universities has greatly increased over the last two decades
   dependent clause: in order to attract students who otherwise might not have gone to a university at all

3 Singular or plural subjects and verbs

Exercise 1

a ✔ ('Government' is a group noun used here to refer to a single unit)
b ✘ (the subject is the plural 'issues')
c ✘ (the subject is the plural 'Problems')
d ✘ (the subject is the plural 'people')
e ✔ (the subject is the plural 'developments')
f ✔ (the subject is the singular 'result')
g ✘ (the subject is the plural 'repercussions')

Exercise 2

a	thinks	e	has
b	tend	f	surround
c	suffer	g	were
d	were		

4 Correct tense formation

Exercise 1

a	✔	d	✔
b	became	e	realised
c	have supported		

Exercise 2

a has
b were
c liked
d had been using
e wore
f owned
g had bought
h were using

i   have become
j   are attracting

5 Using more than one verb tense

Exercise 1

a   ✔
b   had analysed
c   could understand

d   ✔
e   ✔
f   had come

Exercise 2

a   fish **were returning** to the river now that it was unpolluted.
b   he **would stay** in office until the board had appointed a successor.
c   they **were investigating** the problem but had not found the cause yet.
d   the talks **had been successful** and they **hoped** to sign an agreement.
e   until exports rose, economic growth **would not return**.
f   she **could not comment** because she **did not know** the details of the case.

6 Modal verbs

Exercise 1

a   did not need to open
b   had to release
c   cannot
d   need not have resigned
e   must have been working
f   should

Exercise 2

a   Dalio's work in sculpture **could not/cannot have been** a success because she soon turned to painting.
b   With a more attractive design, the product **could have become** a brand leader.
c   Critics argued that the gallery **ought not to have allowed** the painting to be sold to a museum.
d   Fortunately, the organisers **were able to save/managed to save/succeeded in saving** the show by using a back-up generator.

7 Using the passive

Exercise 1

a   The Nobel Peace Prize **was won** by former American President Jimmy Carter in 2002.

b   The Bill **will be debated** by MPs later in the week.
c   The documents **were being destroyed** by a clerk when the police arrived.
d   The referendum **might be postponed** by the Government.
e   Three government buildings **have been occupied** by protestors.
f   Most of the museum's collection **had been stolen** by rioters by the time the army arrived.

Exercise 2

a   It is believed that Walter Clark is the Senate's most skilful debater.
    Walter Clark is believed to be the Senate's most skilful debater.
b   It was reported that two politicians took bribes for their votes.
    Two politicians were reported to have taken bribes for their votes.
c   It is said that talks are taking place between the two parties.
    Talks are said to be taking place between the two parties.
d   It is thought that Che Guevara was executed to avoid the drama of a trial.
    Che Guevara is thought to have been executed to avoid the drama of a trial.

8 Direct and indirect questions

Exercise 1

a   It was hard for legislators at the time to foresee **what the effects of this law would be**.
b   ✔
c   ✔
d   Experts need to co-operate in order to determine exactly **how a new law can be implemented/ how to implement a new law**.
e   Many professionals are still finding out **how the internet affects them** from a professional point of view.
f   ✔
g   The public should be clear about **whether or not they have broken** the law.

Exercise 2

a   We have to ask ourselves **why such a law is required**.
b   It is hard to be exact about **when this problem first arose**.
c   It would be useful to know **what the origins of this law were/how this law originated**.

d People are asking **how quickly the law can be implemented**.

e We have to decide **in what areas/where we should implement this law**.

f The public is asking **what other laws will be needed** in the future.

9 Conditionals (If ...)

Exercise 1

a If Silframe **had increased** their prices, they **would have lost** their share of the youth market.

b Koyley Ltd **might not have failed/might have succeeded** if they **had used** internet marketing.

c The sales team **could have won** new orders if they **had attended** the trade fair in Barcelona.

d If the advertising campaign **had focused on** young professionals, it **would have succeeded**.

e If it **had not diversified** five years ago, Harrtreat plc **would not be flourishing** today.

Exercise 2

a But for	d Even if
b Had the	e If it
c Had it	

Exercise 3

a ✅

b If video links were **to** replace trade fairs, the human link between sales teams and retailers could be lost.

c ✅

d If **it** were not for Gouldnot's successful Paris branch, the company would be making a loss.

e ✅

f Provided **that** it continues to innovate, the company has a bright future.

10 Using adverbs

Exercise 1

a	incredibly	d	✅
b	similarly	e	desperate
c	✅	f	extremely

Exercise 2

a **Astonishingly**, nobody had noticed this problem before. OR Nobody, **astonishingly**, had noticed this problem before.

b Similar research was going on elsewhere, **coincidentally**. OR **Coincidentally**, similar research was going on elsewhere.

c **Unfortunately**, nobody foresaw this problem. OR Nobody foresaw this problem, **unfortunately**.

d **Obviously**, no firm conclusions can be drawn from so little evidence. OR No firm conclusions can be drawn from so little evidence, **obviously.**

e **Apparently/Seemingly**, nothing could have been done to prevent the accident. OR Nothing could have been done to prevent the accident, **apparently/seemingly**.

11 Emphasising

Exercise 1

a It was the one-way system that was making the situation worse.

b What visitors to Scotland enjoy most is its magnificent scenery.

c Only by purchasing local produce can/ will consumers reduce the amount of food transportation.

d What people want is easy access to the main tourist sites.

e It is value for money rather than luxury that most passengers seek in an airline operator.

f Only by retaining their essential character can/ will resorts attract tourism in the long term.

Exercise 2

a	undoubtedly	d	indeed
b	whatsoever	e	entirely
c	itself		

12 Negative words and phrases

Exercise 1

a No sooner had people become accustomed to the situation than it changed.

b No matter how quickly they worked, they could not keep up with demand.

c Hardly had she got rid of one reporter when another one appeared.

d On no account could the policy be allowed to fail.

e It was only when inflation started to rise that people began to worry about the economy.

f Not until recent times has this been considered an important issue.

Exercise 2

a ✅ d ✅
b either e anything
c nor f was it

13 Gerunds and infinitives

Exercise 1

a introducing; to draft
b restructuring; to finalising
c to implement; carrying
d to improve; not to have
e to believe; changing
f to increasing; recruiting

Exercise 2

One of the major problems of his period as Prime Minister was that he could not admit **to making** any mistakes. Aides urged him to do so, on the grounds that it would make the public **think** differently about him. They told him that the public expected their leaders to show a human side, but he refused **to take** any notice of their advice. He would not consider altering his approach and he denied **having** an image that the public found off-putting. For two more years, he tried to justify continuing in the same old way, but eventually the voters had their say.

14 Articles (a/an, the)

Exercise 1

a For most parents, education is one of the biggest sources of concern with regard to their children.
b ✅
c Despite spending large amounts of money, the Government did not manage to achieve its targets for health care.
d It has been argued that people now have higher expectations of life and that this can cause them unhappiness.

Exercise 2

a In 1955, he travelled to India and, on his return, he wrote **an** emotional account of **the** experiences he had had on **the** journey.
b Towards **the** end of **the** 20th century, **the** lives of many people in developed countries were transformed by **the** arrival of computer technology.

c Suddenly, **the** entire industry changed and **a** new approach was required to **the** whole area of marketing.
d There wasn't **an** obvious solution to **the** problem and opinions varied as to **the** best course of action.
e Many people claim in surveys that job satisfaction is more important than **a** high salary.

15 Relative clauses: who, which, that, etc.

Exercise 1

a Much research has been conducted into schizophrenia, **which** causes chronic behavioural problems.
b ✅
c Newton and Einstein are considered to be the scientists to **whom** modern physics owes the greatest debt.
d Water, which may indicate the presence of life, may have existed relatively recently on the surface of Mars.
e ✅

Exercise 2

a A number of questions were asked about the equipment that was used in the experiment.
b The Jodrell Bank Observatory, which was established in 1945, has played an important part in researching meteors, pulsars and quasars.
c John Nash made some of the key early insights into modern game theory, which led to his being co-awarded the Nobel Prize in 1994.
d Michael Faraday was a scientist whose research into magnetic fields gained him his reputation.
e The audience were introduced to Margaret Simons, who had first identified two of the species of spider being discussed.

Exercise 3

a in which
b to whom, to which
c after whom

16 Comparing and contrasting

Exercise 1

a Staff development opportunities are less important to factory employees than clear lines of communication.

b Raw materials can be transported more quickly by train than by road.
c British businesses are not spending as much as European companies on product design, according to recent studies.
d The French engines were heavier than the replacements from Germany.
e Export results are as impressive as import figures this year.
f The safety systems were checked less frequently than they should have been.

Exercise 2

a Kellsver was asked to design a vehicle that would operate in the **wettest** conditions.
b It was not as effective **a** system as the manufacturers had hoped.
c ✅
d Generally speaking, there are **fewer** opportunities for apprenticeships these days.
e If the parts are cooled by water, the process can be completed **sooner**.
f ✅
g Some of the world's most desirable cars are criticised for also being the **least** fuel-efficient.
h The workforce agreed that a shift system was the **safest** way of working.

17 Describing similarities and differences

Exercise 1

a far
b just
c twice as
d one of
e at least

Exercise 2

a Similarly
b differ
c on the contrary
d in common
e In contrast

18 Using noun phrases

Exercise 1

a The **construction of** a one-way system will allow the council to reduce city-centre traffic.
b The chairperson questioned the **relevance of** some of the research.
c There have been **improvements in** the town's provision of cheaper housing in recent years.
d The **specially-adapted** arena will host the athletics contest.

e House prices have risen in the **rapidly-expanding** suburbs.

Exercise 2

a Because of **the likelihood** that residents would object, the proposal was withdrawn.
b The council made final changes to the **carefully-planned** celebrations.
c Local councillors understood **the importance of** the theatre to the town.
d **The widely-held view** was that the council had acted too slowly.

19 Commas (1): correct uses

On 20 July 1969, having stepped onto the Moon's surface, Neil Armstrong uttered the famous words, 'One small step for man, one giant leap for mankind.' Although it had been hoped that the Moon landing would lead to significant advances in space travel, some of which may soon become a reality, scientific progress has generally been slow. However, space research has done much to unite nations. The establishment of the International Space Station, the Space Shuttle and the Hubble Telescope illustrates how much easier and more profitable it is for nations to work as a team, rather than in isolation.

20 Commas (2): incorrect uses

Exercise 1

a As part of the course, you will analyse the theoretical ideas of socialism, conservatism(,) and liberalism.
b The Education Authority, realising that primary and secondary schools in some areas had too many applicants, devised a new admissions policy.
c As the education plan proved to be flawed, impractical and unprofitable, it was quickly abandoned.
d The Government has announced that students who live in rented accommodation are ineligible for financial assistance, whatever their circumstances.
e 'Labelling', the act of saying that a child is of a certain type, usually works to the child's disadvantage.

Exercise 2

According to this week's media, in particular the mainstream newspapers, class sizes in some

British schools in the City of London are too big for Head Teachers to cope with and, as a consequence, some children are not fulfilling their academic potential. As a result of pressure from professionals in education, the Mayor has ordered an official enquiry into the situation, which will be run by Generating Genius, a charitable organisation that has already helped some teenagers from poorer socioeconomic backgrounds to get good university places. The enquiry, which will take place over the next ten months, will look into a range of educational issues, including overcrowding in classrooms, improving overall standards, and promoting relationships between state and independent schools. On 12th November, the Mayor will speak at the Institute of Education, where, in the words of one reporter, 'there will be considerable interest in what he has to say'. In the meantime, in order to ensure that class sizes do not get out of hand, it is possible that the Greater London Authority will take steps to alleviate the situation by, for example, allocating some of its own buildings to the education of its city's young people.

21 Colons and semicolons

Exercise 1

a   The report focuses on three issues: how reliable public transport systems are; what measures would be most effective in reducing traffic congestion; and whether parking facilities are adequate.

b   Most reports on the inner city focus on problems; in fact there have been many improvements too.

c   This leads us to an important development in town planning: the arrival of out-of-town shopping centres.

d   Tomlinson was correct when he made the statement: 'Urban planners should always aim to avoid demolishing historic buildings'.

e   Among town planners today, there is one buzzword: sustainability.

Exercise 2

a   This brings me to my final point: the repercussions of these initiatives have not been fully considered.

b   The drive to create a sustainable environment raises a serious question: to what extent should function take precedence over form?

c   People who argue that cities are becoming overcrowded should ask themselves why.

d   In some societies, homes need to be built to accommodate a range of family structures, including extended families, nuclear families and single-parent households.

22 Hyphens, dashes and brackets

Exercise 1

a   This was a **well-received** reform at the time. Prior to that change, only **upper-class** people had been able to vote.

b   The records were not up to date and an **old-fashioned** system was still in place.

c   His **co-defendant** in the case was his former boss, and after a **three-month** trial they were both found guilty.

d   By the time he was thirty years old, he had a **high-powered** job advising the Government on **state-run** services.

e   Countries wanted **self-determination** and the status of being fully independent.

Exercise 2

a   Opponents questioned the logic of his argument – much to his annoyance.

b   He made a speech in the House of Commons – and this was not the only time when he went against his own party – in which he heavily criticised the policy.

c   Mistakes were made, inefficiency dogged the entire project, and complaints came in from all sides – this was not how things were supposed to be.

d   Pensioners – regardless of their personal and financial circumstances – were all better off because of this change.

Exercise 3

a   There were exceptions to this pattern but the results were generally very consistent. (Exceptions are listed in the table below.) It was therefore possible to draw firm conclusions.

b   He was a strong supporter of entry into the eurozone and played a significant role in the country's decision to take that step. (He later regretted this, but that was far in the future.)

c   In her influential report (*Approaches to Poverty*, 2020), Browne proposed wholesale changes to welfare rules.

d   The unforeseen consequence (fewer workers having job security) seriously affected morale in the industry.

23   Apostrophes

Exercise 1

a   The beneficial effect of Vitamin D on **children's** health has been noted in recent research findings.

b   Apparently, **Ferrari's** latest supercar can reach speeds of over 200 miles per hour.

c   The development of **teenagers'** identities is heavily influenced by their **peers'** behaviour.

d   People have enjoyed **Beethoven's** music for more than 200 years.

e   **I've** always believed that a **designer's** approach should be to follow his or her intuition, rather than **clients'** ideas.

Exercise 2

a   Sales of **DVDs** rose rapidly during the period, and **their** ascendancy over **videos** was soon confirmed.

b   Cinema-going reached its height in the **1940s**, when its escapist appeal attracted audiences wanting to see movie stars **whose** lives seemed incredibly glamorous.

c   Boeing 747s are popular commercial aircraft, and many **millions** of travellers have used them.

d   Research into people in their **20s** indicates that **theirs** is the first generation to be confronted by this problem, and many of them **can't** find a way to deal with it.

24   Inverted commas

Exercise 1

a   'There are many different ways of accessing the information,' the manual stated.

b   In a letter to his family, he wrote: 'The thought has struck me that perhaps the artistic life is not for me.'

c   ✓

d   'Why do certain people have these behaviour patterns?' she asks at the beginning of her paper.

e   ✓

f   One expert stated that the situation 'would not improve significantly … for a considerable period of time'.

Exercise 2

a   In his paper 'The Impact of the Internet', he argued that too little attention was being paid to what he called 'the sudden intrusion'. By this he meant the speed at which the internet took over people's lives. 'These days,' he said, 'people have lost the ability to think for themselves and to use their own initiative.'

b   After the first day of conference, the leaders announced in their official statement: 'We feel that we have made significant progress towards a solution on this difficult question.' They also spoke of the 'extremely cordial relations we enjoy'. 'We anticipate a further announcement after tomorrow's negotiations,' they added.

25   Capital letters

Exercise

a   Due to the screening of the **Mexican Grand Prix**, this week's quiz show, '**Send** a **Line**', will be broadcast on **ITV** at the earlier time of 5.00 pm on **Friday**.

b   Farmers in the **Ivory Coast** live in poverty, while the cocoa they produce feeds the world's chocolate industry.

c   The folk artist, **Steve Knightly**, mixes music and legend on his **CD**, '**Cruel River**'.

d   Students wishing to go to university in **North America** are advised to take the **International Baccalaureate**.

e   The flood seriously affected homes in the north-west of England and completely destroyed the 100-year-old premises of **Grandacre** and **Sons** in **Preston**.

f   Last week, the **UK Border Agency** announced that it would be making a number of changes in line with the **Government's** new policies.

g   The **Renaissance** was a period when great developments took place across **Europe** in art and literature.

h   In her paper, '**Talking** in **Twos**', **Amanda Pritchard** examines a new approach to raising bilingual children.

26 Linking: contrasting

Exercise 1

a Whilst the number of annual visitors to the Galapagos Islands was 41,000 in 1991, it is now around 170,000.

b Despite optimistic economic predictions, business confidence has fallen over the past few months. OR Business confidence has fallen over the past few months, despite optimistic economic predictions.

c Weather data has been collected in Britain for 350 years. However, opinions differ on how reliable that data is. OR Opinions differ, however, on how reliable that data is. OR Opinions differ on how reliable that data is, however.

d Even though a dispersant was sprayed onto the oil slick, thousands of seabirds were washed up along the beach.

e Some businesses invest heavily in researching new products, whereas others prefer to allocate more funds to marketing. OR Whereas some businesses invest heavily in researching new products, others prefer to allocate more funds to marketing.

Exercise 2

a It is a well-known fact that conservation projects can be costly. Nevertheless, they need to be prioritised.

b Although some parents believe in the benefits of home tutoring, most think that children require the school environment for the full development of their social skills.

c In spite of the warnings given by the medical profession, people still smoke. OR In spite of the fact that the medical profession gives warnings, people still smoke. OR In spite of receiving warnings from the medical profession, people still smoke.

d Social-networking sites were designed to develop new friendships. However, their main use has been to communicate within existing peer groups. OR Social-networking sites were designed to develop new friendships. Their main use, however, has been to communicate with existing peer groups.

e Whilst most film festivals in the world show one or two German movies, films 'Made in Germany' are not given the recognition they deserve.

27 Linking: adding

Exercise 1

a Raw materials are becoming more expensive. In addition, the costs of transporting them are increasing. OR In addition to raw materials becoming more expensive, the costs of transporting them are increasing.

b As well as improving staff performance, staff-development opportunities increase employees' loyalty.

c Not only is Zolltrack winning contracts in the private sector, but it is also having success in the public sector.

d A new recruitment process was introduced, with impressive results.

e Changing the factory's layout would be expensive. It could, furthermore, delay production.

f Having so far done most of its business in the UK, Zolltrack is now operating in America as well.

Exercise 2

a Not only was ACYG Solutions declared bankrupt, but also its CEO was given a six-year prison sentence for fraud.

b As well as making record profits in 2011, GVCY won an award for its staff-development programme.

c Zolltrack's braking system is the most technologically advanced on the market. Moreover, at the moment, its system is also the cheapest. OR At the moment, moreover, its system is also the cheapest.

d Cornyt streamlined its management structure, with 52 middle managers being made redundant.

e Grupmot plc has increased its market share in the UK in addition to winning new contracts in Spain.

28 Linking: causes

Exercise 1

a Crime rates have risen in this part of the city, **which** is why so many residents have sold up and left.

b On account of the museum **being** able to attract private sponsorship, their short-term future seems secure.

c The media's new power to question and criticise may have brought **about** a lack of respect for politicians.

d The research facility was closed because **of** serious concerns about its standards of health and safety.

e One reason **for** an episode of hyperactivity in children may be the excessive consumption of sugar.

f A number of basic errors were made due to **the fact that** no trained medical staff were present at the time. OR A number of basic errors were made **due to no trained staff being present** at the time.

Exercise 2

a Since many citizens are dissatisfied with the way in which lobbyists influence government policy, there are often calls for reform.

b Some adolescents appear to suffer from headaches and anxiety due to their repeated poor performance in computer games.

c On the grounds that it would affect their trade, local shopkeepers attacked the new parking charge. OR Local shopkeepers attacked the new parking charge on the grounds that it would affect their trade.

d Syms argues that a period of mental illness may be triggered by an apparently trivial event.

29 Linking: results

Exercise 1 (sample answers)

a Unemployment in the region was **so** high that the Government felt obliged to establish an enterprise zone.

b The digital revolution has led **to** a much wider range of programme choices for the consumer.

c Accidents in laboratories may result **from** a lack of supervision.

d Funding for the arts fell. **Therefore**, many groups and organisations were unable to continue.

e Employment opportunities in the sector fell, **resulting** in increased competition for jobs.

f Dickens regularly gave talks and readings, thereby **raising** his public profile.

Exercise 2

a Both of the town's electronics factories were forced to close during the recession. As a result, the only employment opportunities to be found are in the service and public sectors. OR Both of the town's electronics factories were forced to close during the recession, as a result of which the only employment opportunities to be found are in the service and public sectors. OR Both of the town's electronics factories were forced to close during the recession and, as a result, the only employment opportunities to be found are in the service and public sectors.

b Riots continued for ten days, which meant that many villages were left in ruins.

c Radiation leaks at the Chernobyl plant resulted from the absence of a confinement shell.

d Seasonal Affective Disorder (SAD) seems to stem from a shortage of sunlight.

30 Signposting

Exercise 1

a preceding
b latter, following
c above
d former

Exercise 2

a In the paragraph **above**, we saw how Milan emerged as Italy's most important commercial centre.

b After Paris, Lyon and Marseille are the second and third biggest cities in France **respectively**. OR After Paris, Lyon and Marseille are, **respectively**, the second and third biggest cities in France.

c By exploring the statistics in the table **below**, it will be possible to appreciate the scale of Germany's postwar recovery.

d There is a certain amount of rivalry between Madrid and Barcelona. **The former** is the centre of power, while **the latter** often regards itself as the economic driving force of the country.

31 Using pronouns correctly

Exercise 1

a Senior managers took their staff to a hotel, where **the managers/the former** gave presentations.

b To do **his or her** job well, a human resources manager needs imagination as well as knowledge of procedures. OR To do their job well, human-resources managers need imagination as well as knowledge of procedures.

c The conference on performance management ended with a keynote speech. **The speech/ The latter** was a great success, according to those who attended.

d A council of student representatives was formed and **its** task was to liaise with the student body.

Exercise 2

a warnings

b trend

c measures

d phenomenon

32 Avoiding repetition of words

Exercise 1

a Most young people make compromises with their parents that allow the family to work as an entity, but some teenagers seem unable to **do so/do this**.

b The two housing trusts decided to merge in 2020. **Both** believed that working together would improve outcomes.

c Of all the charities working with homeless people, the **one** whose name is most familiar to the public is Shelter.

d There have been many attempts to renovate empty housing stock and make it available to families in need. The **latest** (one) has been sponsored by the property group Campton Holdings.

e Stableton Ltd agreed in 2016 to improve the living conditions of its 540 tenants in Islington, but when an inspection took place in 2018, it was evident that it had not **done so**.

Exercise 2 (sample answer)

The charity Homes for People invested some of its savings in a business with a scheme for contructing ecological housing on a site outside Leeds. The **location** for the **project** seemed ideal, but it became apparent after six months that very **few homes** *were* actually being **built**. When the charity contacted the **company** to establish why **half a year** had elapsed without any obvious progress, it discovered that the entire **venture** had been sub-contracted to a smaller **firm**.

33 Parallel structures

Exercise 1

a to promote/deal with/monitor

b have/know

c an increase/a fall

d meet/play/is

e using/going through

Exercise 2 (sample answers)

a The course syllabus includes **an analysis of** the concept of innovation, **the design/ designing of** technical images and **the preparation of** project specifications.

b The music entitled 'Before Dawn' **was written** by Dominique Ferris and **published** in 2010.

c The research will investigate the number of people **leaving** school early and **getting** married.

d Equipment **has to be bought**, laboratories **set up** and **staff hired** before any work can begin.

e Global air travel is **safe**, **convenient** and more **fuel-efficient** than it used to be.

Exercise 3 (sample answers)

a Teamwork is beneficial because it involves **mixing** with different types of people, **pooling** ideas and **reaching** joint decisions.

b A successful marketing strategy needs **clear objectives**, **a wide-ranging advertising campaign** and **strong public support**.

34 Participles

Exercise 1

a ('a new model' is not the subject of 'spotting')

b ✅

c ('he' is not the subject of 'written').

d ✅

e ('the proposed merger' is not the subject of 'sought')

f ✅

Exercise 2 (sample answers)

a **Having carried out** extensive market research, they launched the new product./ They carried out market research before **launching** the new product.

b **Wishing** to streamline the operation, the management reduced staffing.

c **Overtaken/Having been overtaken** by competitors in terms of market share, the company had to respond quickly.

d The garage, **experiencing** keen competition from other companies, began to struggle.

e **Having drawn up** a shortlist of candidates, the officers passed it to the manager for review.

f Customer satisfaction, **monitored** by in-store complaints records, rose to an all time high during the holiday period.

Exercise 3 (sample answers)

a **Having lost** market share, Jagsta plc made 100 staff redundant. **Operating** as a smaller company, it returned to profitability.

b Bulltop Construction Ltd, **founded** in 2008, grew quickly. **Having landed** a major public sector contract in 2009, the company moved to new premises.

35 Incomplete sentences

Exercise 1

a ✗ d ✗
b ✓ e ✗
c ✓ f ✓

Exercise 2 (sample answers)

a All sentences apart from the first one should be underlined.
The jury system is a central plank of the British legal system. **However, there are** a number of its critics who say that it is outdated **and that** many cases are too complex for ordinary members of the public. **As a result**, they feel that juries should not be used any longer.

b The first and last sentences should be underlined.
There are a number of reasons why the ruling party might lose the next election **and** the state of the economy is probably the top one. **As** many people are losing their jobs and businesses are unable to attract investment, **there is** a growing loss of faith in the Government.

c The last two sentences should be underlined.
A backbench MP can rise to prominence **if** he or she makes an exceptional speech **which** is reported in the press or if he or she chairs a committee, particularly when **it** interviews public figures.

d All sentences apart from the first one should be underlined.
TV watchers could not believe how many people the protest attracted, **despite the fact that it was** one of the wettest days of the year. On every street in the city centre there were hundreds of protestors, **carrying** slogans and **denouncing** the Government's policies.

36 Avoiding long and disorganised sentences

Exercise 1 (sample answers)

a Studies of youth culture in Britain always tend to focus on the 1960s as that is the period when many changes were clearly visible in British society and when the whole subject became a matter of public debate. **However**, many of these developments actually began in the 1950s and any study of youth culture should really begin in that decade.

b The difference between sociological and journalistic approaches to events is that in the first approach sociologists have to use scientific methods to gather their information. Journalists, **on the other hand**, can easily make up information without witnessing the actual event, which sometimes makes them biased.

c Prime Ministers are like senior managers in that they can delegate much of their power to individual departments, focusing their energy on overall strategy and presentation. **Another approach is that** they can micro-manage the individual decisions of their department heads, but if they choose this route, they risk being overwhelmed by the sheer scale of modern government.

Exercise 2 (sample answers)

a George Orwell is chiefly known for his novels *Animal Farm* and *Nineteen Eighty-Four* and these are still widely read today. **In addition**, he wrote a great deal of important journalism, for example *Road to Wigan Pier* about the life of miners and the relevance of socialism.

b

c It has been argued, with the benefit of graphic anecdotes, that organisations are hampered by health and safety legislation. **However**, when individual elements of the law are closely examined, it becomes clear that it is an exaggerated interpretation by managers that is causing the problem, rather than the code itself.

37 Avoiding too many short sentences

Exercise 1 (sample answers)

a The silent film era, **which** began in the late 19th century, continued until the 1920s **when** recorded sound became possible.

b Politicians have become more and more reliant on focus groups, **which** came into existence in the 1990s **and** involve **carefully selected groups** of people giving their views on political issues.

c Large hospitals can be cost-effective **by moving** staff members **who** are underemployed in their part of the building to an area of greater need.

d A small restaurant **that** has ambitions to expand may decide to make an offer on adjacent premises **and in** this way it gains the additional space it requires.

e The research team, **initially criticised** for making slow progress, was actually involved in a fundamental rethinking of domestic heating systems, **which** would lead to an innovative and successful design.

Exercise 2 (sample answers)

a The Industrial Revolution, **which** transformed the entire world, could be said to have started in Derbyshire and Shropshire, two counties in the north Midlands. Arkwright's Wheel, **which** used water power for the spinning of cotton, was invented in Derbyshire in 1771 **and** the Iron Bridge in Shropshire, **built** in 1781, was the first arch bridge made of cast iron.

b Michael Cimino submitted a script for *Heaven's Gate*, **then called** *The Johnson County War*, to United Artists in 1971. **Having failed** to attract attract high-profile actors, the project was shelved until 1979, **when** it began shooting with a budget of $11.6 million, **which** had risen to $30 million by the time the film was finished.

38 Building successful long sentences

Exercise (sample answers)

a Sports psychology is based on the belief **that** many top competitors are of similar ability and **that** what separates winners from losers is their state of mind **and** their ability to meet the mental challenge as well as the physical one.

b The 1990s was a very significant period in terms of the country's development, **as** the national economy grew more quickly than ever before and there were **also** a number of social changes **that** resulted in various problems.

c Files stored long-term on computers are easy to access and require little storage space, **but** there is a danger that, years or even decades later, the data may be unreadable by a malfunctioning machine **for which** spare parts are no longer available.

39 Hedging (1)

Exercise 1

a The latest rise in unemployment **could weaken** consumer confidence in the economy.

b Resistance to innovation **tends to come** from a fear of change.

c Smaller electronics companies **seemed to be** outperforming their larger rivals.

d Greater regulation of banking practice **would help to enhance** the reputation of the financial sector.

e The evidence **indicates** that stricter regulation of online loan companies is required.

f Even 'scientific' decision-making **may be shaped** by the personal values of the decision-maker.

g The practice of 'short selling' **contributed to** the collapse of Lehman Brothers.

Exercise 2

a arguably
b apparently
c rarely
d probably
e normally

40 Hedging (2)

Exercise 1

a **It is estimated that** 80% of Quapaw Native Americans died from a smallpox virus introduced by European settlers.

b High levels of stress at work **are likely to lead** to illness.

c Exercise is important **in that** it may improve mental health.

d Although it is still being trialled, **it can be/ could be/has been argued that** this new antibiotic will have better long-term prospects.

e The public health campaign was successful **in terms of** raising awareness of the issue.

Exercise 2

a PFIs in the public health sector have suffered to **some** extent from poor project management.

b Restructuring these two hospitals will, **in** principle, improve their performance.

c The treatment was successful insofar **as** it alleviated the symptoms.

d It has **been** claimed that people who live alone take longer to recover from some illnesses.

e In the area of mental health, patients recover more quickly, as **a** rule, if they receive counselling as well as medication.

Exercise 3 (sample answer)

The latest research **indicates** that poor diet is a major factor in a number of serious illnesses. **It could be argued that** the Government must therefore increase the amount of money it spends on education programmes. Improving the nation's diet **is likely to be** cost-effective because it will reduce expenditure on the NHS. Fewer ill employees **could** also represent a significant saving to business by minimising the incidence of sick leave.

41 Giving a definition

Exercise 1 (sample answers)

a An avatar **is**/**was** defined by Spinrad in *Songs from the Stars* (1980) as a …

b A digital immigrant is a person **who** was born before the start of the digital age.

c Data mining is a process **by which**/**whereby** a company develops profiles …

d A computer virus is a program (such as the Conficker worm) **that can reproduce itself and be transmitted between computers**. (The Conficker worm is an example, not a definition.)

e Apple Inc. **is an American corporation that** produces and sells consumer electronics, personal computers and computer software.

f A mouse is a **device** for controlling the movement of a cursor on a computer screen.

Exercise 2 (sample answers)

a Cyber bullying describes the use of online facilities to torment specific individuals.

b Wikipedia is an online encyclopedia whose entries are written by volunteers.

c Globalisation could be defined as the process whereby international financial and cultural systems become more uniform.

d A USB flash drive is a small device for storing data separately from a personal computer.

e A chat room is an online forum that allows a group of participants to communicate with each other in real time.

42 Introducing an example

Exercise 1

a how difficult it can be to pump groundwater

b A range of educational activities

c complications

d laws … designed to protect waterways and land from degradation

e traditional approaches to enhancing crop performance

Exercise 2 (sample answers)

a This can improve many people's quality of life by, *for example*, enabling them to have a better diet.

b i.e. should be e.g.

c Some statistics on organic farming can be surprising, for example, *those related to* sugar cane. (Sugar cane is not a statistic.)

d

Exercise 3

a example (not illustration)

b Take

c such

d illustrated/exemplified

e An/One

43 Citing

Exercise 1

a As Jennings **states**: 'The home is of paramount importance.'

b No one really knew what term to use, until Mo (1995) **came** up with the expression, 'blue hour'.

c ✔

d Barton (2018) **says/points out/notes/** etc. that few people really understand the problem.

e Green *et al.* **argue** that price is always a factor.

f ✔

g ✔

h According to Pine-Smith (2005), 'we have to take into account the child's home environment'.

Exercise 2

a ✔

b Compliance is a critical factor (Peters, 2013; Lilley, 1999).

c ✔

d While nobody can challenge this idea, 'other areas of a child's life also play their part' (Fielding, 2004).

e Grahams (2019) insists that 'this old notion has to be rejected once and for all'.

44 Paraphrasing

Exercise 1 (sample answers)

a must/have to; open-mindedness/broad-mindedness/understanding

b condemned/denounced; cruel/inhuman/brutal

c Legislation/Regulations; stop/halt; enthusiastically/unreservedly

d energetically/vigorously; harmful/deleterious

Exercise 2 (sample answers)

a The report advised the charity to make the range of its projects more extensive.

b 'Compassion fatigue' can result from an excess of disaster campaigns.

c It is essential that aid workers are familiar with local customs.

d Despite raising enough money, FoodAid was unable to get supplies to the region.

Exercise 3 (sample answers)

a Myers (2019) argues that the success of an aid advertisement depends on providing the public with key facts on the local situation as well as arousing sympathy.

b According to Davis (2021), the Government will probably maintain its international aid spending despite its efforts to reduce the deficit.

c Briggs (2011) notes that charities are currently competing more intensely than ever.

45 Incorporating data

Exercise 1

a conducted
b analysed
c differences
d significant
e consistent
f reached

Exercise 2

a participants
b conducted
c aim
d predicted
e difference
f variation
g results
h observations
i finding

46 Formal language (1)

Exercise 1 (sample answers)

a One **advertisement** in a successful campaign shows a young **father** in a park, who is looking after **two children**, and who fails to notice some of the dangers present in the situation.

b In the promotion of their food products, some companies **seem to ignore** the health risks for children.

c Encouraging young people to think that it is **socially acceptable** to become drunk is **morally questionable**.

d If young people suspect that they are being patronised, they may **make every effort to** avoid the campaign message.

e The problem of overeating **will not be resolved** by health campaigns on their own. OR … **will not be resolved solely** by health campaigns.

Exercise 2 (sample answers)

a There is a persuasive argument for banning food and drink advertisements that target children under ten.

b It has to be recognised that a car can play an important role in a person's sense of autonomy.

c It seems preferable for the food industry to regulate itself in the area of advertising, rather than for new laws to be created.

d There has been a demand among consumers for information about the food and drink that they purchase.

e There can be little doubt that young people are now much more aware of the dangers of alcohol abuse. OR It seems clear that …

47 Formal language (2)

Exercise 1

a An enquiry has been initiated into (the) voting irregularities that seem to have occurred in the north of the region.

b A brief consultation took place between the President and the leader of the majority party, before the latter was pronounced Prime Minister. OR After a brief consultation between the President and the leader of the majority party, the latter was pronounced Prime Minister.

c A series of laws was enacted to grant religious freedom to the population.

d Monitors had to ensure that polling stations were accessible to all the adults in the region.

Exercise 2 (sample answers)

a … successfully **addressed** the major problems …

b Objections … were **negligible**. OR There were **few** objections …

c A **de facto** leader …

d … political freedom and **vice versa**.

e … resulting in a **pro rata** reduction …

48 The language of argument

Exercise (sample answer)

This essay will start by defining the term 'globalisation'. Next it will consider some of the drawbacks of this process in the developing world, and examine claims that globalisation brings about a loss of cultural identity. In the second half, the essay will describe some political gains that international integration may have contributed to, and explore the recent success of a number of international campaigns. Finally, it will conclude that, on balance, globalisation has helped rather than hindered humankind.

49 The language of critique

Exercise 1

a Harry Harlow was criticised **for** using rhesus macaque monkeys in his isolation experiments.

b Another problem **with** the case study method is that it is susceptible to researcher bias.

c The proposed review might be more instructive **if** it referred to Popper's criticism of psychoanalysis.

d Dewey is praised **by** Forster for integrating psychology with social issues.

e The notion that free will is an illusion **is** challenged in Gray's article.

f The study would **have** been more illuminating if it had taken social settings into account.

Exercise 2

a Beck (1994) **supports** the view that CBT has been effective for treating depression.

b Piaget (1936) was the first psychologist to **make a systematic** study of cognitive development.

c Klein was **innovative in** both her techniques and her theories on infant development.

d Titchener created **a ground-breaking** psychology programme at Cornell University.

e Bloch upholds **the claim that** Watzlawick's insights into communication were revolutionary.

f Sturges and Briony **question the** idea that subjective experiences are the only way to study human behaviour.

g Lemchok's work appears **to overlook** the distinction between competence and performance.

50 Using prepositions (1)

Exercise 1

a about/over, of
b of, in, with
c with, of
d in, on
e for, to

Exercise 2

a This is the area about which we have most knowledge.

b Here are the results on which I based my assessment.

c The survey identified individuals for whom there is no current provision.

d You need to look at the groups into which the insects have been classified.

e Sometimes there are problems for which we do not have explanations.

f   It turned out to be a situation from which most people benefited.

51 Using prepositions (2)

Exercise 1

a found	d research
b to	e consists of
c apart from	f in

Exercise 2

a regard	e retrospect
b keeping/line	f terms
c view/opinion	g exception
d account	h light

52 Creating longer words

Exercise 1

a   likelihood, uncertainty, strengthened/ strengthens, expansion
b   contributor, environmental, unstoppable
c   assessment, outdated, underperform
d   probability, technological, transformation
e   characterised, disappointingly, unimaginative, leadership

Exercise 2 (sample answer)

There was **disagreement** among people as to which course of action would be the most **effective**. The company's founders felt **passionately** that their position was the correct one and they were **unsympathetic** towards the views of others. This **exemplifies** the kind of struggle that was going on within many organisations at the time.

Exercise 3

a disheartening	g irrespective
b illogical	h disorderly
c unjustifiable	i inconsistent
d underestimate	j unnatural
e inconceivable	k illegal
f non-compliant	l impure

53 Using single words for impact

Exercise 1

a Undoubtedly	c misunderstood
b incomprehensible	d immeasurable

Exercise 2

a   variable
b   highlighted

c   infrastructure
d   bankruptcy/bankruptcies
e   Inflationary

54 Using phrasal verbs

Exercise 1 (sample answers)

a   It may take a small business more than a year to **recover from** a quarterly fall in sales.
b   During the train strike, Edgo plc **provided** a special bus service to take employees from the factory to the head office.
c   A tier of middle managers were **made redundant**, and six junior staff were appointed to replace them.
d   In times of recession, companies often **reduce the number of** seasonal and temporary staff.
e   Some consumers are likely to feel they are being **exploited**/**cheated** if the monthly cost of calls rises dramatically.
f   **Communicating** your ideas in a concise way is the key to success in a presentation.
g   A meeting was called in an attempt to **resolve** the dispute.

Exercise 2

a   set up
b   speak out
c   weighing up
d   drew on
e   called for
f   hold up

55 Collocations (1)

Exercise 1

a   stability
b   influence
c   firmly
d   impact
e   focus
f   highly
g   widely

Exercise 2

a   increasingly
b   carefully
c   clearly
d   critically
e   closely

f privately

g highly

56 Collocations (2)

Exercise 1

a contribution

b assessment

c access

d benefits

e awareness

f causes

g role

Exercise 2

a environment

b grants

c problems

d findings

e gathering

f outcome

57 Commonly misused words

Exercise 1

a emigrants e infer

b imminent f economic

c assured g complimentary

d lose h is composed

Exercise 2

a incident e effect

b elicit f averse

c ensure g apprised

d advice h historic

58 Commonly confused words – homonyms

Exercise 1

a Principle e passed

b too costly f ✔

c ✔ g whether

d allowed h bear

Exercise 2

a your paying – you are/you're paying

b whose receiving – who is/who's receiving

c their trustworthy – they are/they're trustworthy

d its impossible – it is/it's impossible

e wether – whether

f whose been – who has/who's been

g you're faith – your faith

h their as – there as

i there game – their game

j it's advantages – its advantages

59 Key spelling rules

Exercise 1

a	controlling	'control' ends in vowel + 'l', so the final consonant should be doubled
b	diaries	'diary' ends in 'y', so change this to 'ie' when forming the plural
c	misquoted	'quoted' does not begin with 's', so the letter should be singular
d	hygienic	the suffix is '-ic', so the final 'e' is dropped
e	delightful	the suffix '-ful' never has double 'l'
f	irregular	the 'ir-' prefix requires double 'r'
g	biddable	'bid' is a word ending vowel + consonant, so the final consonant should be doubled before the suffix is added
h	disappointed	in this case, there is no double letter with the 'dis-' prefix

Exercise 2

a openness, improvement

b primarily, stressful

c co-operation, noticeable

d arguments, misconstrued

e setting, achievement

f continuities, awaiting

g companies, prohibited

h behaviour, dissimilar

60 Common spelling mistakes

Exercise 1

a	weird	f	opportunities
b	necessary	g	✔
c	commitment	h	✔
d	✔	i	successful
e	stabilise	j	conceive

Exercise 2

Corrections
accomplished
religious
contemporaries
realities
knowledge
primarily
characters
portray
pessimistic

61 Writing an email to your tutor (sample answers)

Use correct grammar

Subject: Request for extension, Tony Hill, Social Studies, 2036

I'm really sorry but I'll be late handing in my assignment on care of the elderly. The due date's **the** 27th of this month and I know I **should have** finished by then but I wonder if I **can/could** hand it in a week later. I've been off sick with a really bad throat infection and **haven't had** time to do all the reading yet. I'd like to ask for a week's extension, **which** would give me time to catch up. I hope my term grades **won't be** affected by this.

Punctuate your email

I've just started the module on **World** Archaeology (3033) and am finding the topic a bit too broad. I realise that, although I like the global coverage, I would be better suited to something more specific. **As** I've always had an interest in African Archaeology, could I change to this module?

Make clear connections within sentences

Subject: Sponsorship – Mongol Rally – Dave Couch

I've decided to take part in the Mongol Rally next year, **which** involves driving a car from Europe to Mongolia over the summer vacation. I wonder if you'd be willing to sponsor me for **this event/activity**? It's not a race and I'm not trying to win anything – **it's** all about making it to the end of the route and donating your vehicle to a local charity. I've always admired **those** people who take on a charitable cause, so I've decided to have a go at **it/one** myself. May I count on your support?

Make sure your sentences can be understood

I'd like to change the topic for my presentation. I did say that I would do it on communication issues, **having previously worked** on this. But I've found it very hard to find enough material or **get** the right ideas. Now I think I have a better idea that I've been working on. **Is it** okay if I do it on sensory deprivation instead?

Make sure style and function are appropriate

Subject: Re our appointment

I've just realised that I should have been meeting with you this morning! I **don't know** why I forgot but **I'm really sorry about it**. I'd like to re-schedule the meeting if possible **because** I still have some problems with my presentation. **Would Friday at 10 be possible**?

Use appropriate words and correct spelling

I've just applied for a job as a volunteer in a charity shop and I need to provide the names of two people who know me but who aren't relatives. I'd really **appreciate** it if I could put **your** name down as a **referee**. I think they'll contact you and it only **involves** writing a short paragraph about me, outlining my skills and giving some information about my **character**. I don't think there's any **point in** writing a lot as it's only a **temporary** job.

Could I also contact you for **advice** if I get an interview?

62 Covering letters and CVs

Exercise 1

a I am keen to gain experience in the world of **p**ublishing, **which** is why I am writing to you. (OR I am writing to you **because** I am keen to gain experience in the world of **p**ublishing.)

b Having worked as a receptionist in a busy GP practi**c**e, I believe I would respond well to the pressures of the post.

c My CV, which you will find enclosed, lists the various positions that I **held** from 2017 to 2020, while I was a member of the student **council.**

d In the **past** three years at college, not only **have I** taken evening classes in Chinese, but I have also made two trips to Beijing to visit **c**omputer **t**rade **f**airs.

Exercise 2

a **Handling** customer complaints was the most important part of this part-time post.

b 2018–2020   Rumworth Sixth Form College, Leicester
A Levels: Maths (A*), Physics (A), Biology (B), French (C).

c Working as part of **P**rofessor Robertson's research group helped me to develop comp**l**e**m**entary skills in communication and teamwork**, w**hich proved useful when I organised a presentation on our findings. (OR … and teamwork. These proved …)

d Having a good knowledge of recent trends in online shopping **is** vital, in my view, to the **r**etail **i**ndustry**,** which is why my **final-year** dissertation focused on **people's** reasons for switching from popular **high-street** outlets to internet retail sites.

Index

References are to page numbers.
Entries in *italic type* indicate words or phrases whose use is illustrated and explained.
Numbers in **bold type** indicate pages on which the indexed grammatical term is a main topic.